AND WHILE I HAVE BEEN LYING HERE PERFECTLY STILL

THE SASKIA OLDE WOLBERS FILES

PHILIP MONK

Art Gallery of York University

Library and Archives Canada Cataloguing in Publication

Olde Wolbers, Saskia, 1971-
    And while I have been lying here perfectly still : the
Saskia Olde Wolbers files / by Philip Monk; edited by
Michael Maranda; designed by Bryan Gee.

Includes bibliographical references.
Catalogue of an exhibition held at the Art Gallery of York
    University, Toronto, Ont. from Feb. 6 - May 4, 2008.

ISBN 978-0-921972-53-2

I. Monk, Philip, 1950- II. Maranda, Michael, 1966- III. York
University (Toronto, Ont.). Art Gallery IV. Title.

N6953.O44A4 2009   778.59092   C2009-900507-7

Available through:
D.A.P. / Distributed Art Publishers
155 Sixth Avenue, 2nd Floor
New York NY 10013
Tel: (212) 627-1999
Fax: (212) 627-9484

Table of Contents

Case Studies

Exhibition

Case Studies

Russell Clergy

EDITED BY STANLEY PUGH, PhD

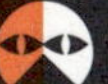

*THE CASE
STUDIES
OF RUSSELL
CLERGY*

THE CASE STUDIES OF RUSSELL CLERGY

PSEUDOLOGIA

I am aware that – in this town, at least –
there are many physicians who (revolting
though it may seem) choose to read a case
history of this kind not as a contribution
to the psychopathology of neuroses, but as
a *roman à clef* designed for their private
delectation. I can assure readers of this
species that every case history which I may
have occasion to publish in the future will
be secured against their perspicacity by
similar guarantees of secrecy, even though
this resolution is bound to put quite
extraordinary restrictions on my choice
of material.

– SIGMUND FREUD
"Fragment of an Analysis of a Case of Hysteria"

Forward
Florence Wellington, MD

I came across these case studies in my husband's papers: the most enigmatic that he left. Of course, the term "case studies" seems a misnomer for this confused series of speculations. Confused, I say advisedly: not only in the disorder of thought displayed – it's as if he fell victim to what he was studying – but also in the material itself. To clarify, we cannot be certain whether they refer to one or several cases and, indeed, whether some are not fictions, that is, counterfeit cases. Furthermore, we do not know whether there is one subject to whom we can attribute these analyses. "S. O. W." says the banker's box containing a number of files – whether initials of a name, we cannot say. (For a moment, I was startled wondering whether these initials were a scrambling of O. W. S., those of neurologist Oliver W. Sacks, the author of his own popular series of case studies, but this is unlikely since my husband had no association with him.) Individually, these files are labelled *Placebo*, *Interloper*, *Kilowatt Dynasty*, *Trailer*, and *Deadline*. The box also contains a number of DVDs with corresponding titles.

If only in his case studies my husband had been as diligent in his concatenation of material as Freud was when the latter wrote, "In the face of the incompleteness of my analytic results, I had no choice but to follow the example of those discoverers whose good fortune it is to bring to the light of day after their long burial the priceless though mutilated relics of antiquity. I have restored what is missing, taking the best models known to me from other analyses; but like a conscientious archaeologist I have not omitted to mention in each case where the authentic parts end and my constructions begin." In the fragmentary state in which the documents published here were left, it is not a matter of a competent editor identifying the links and providing the unacknowledged sources. For these "sources" may have been a deliberate attempt at misrepresentation, indeed, of fictional inspiration. At times, I have had the uncanny sensation of reading a case study as if written by Edgar Allan Poe. That, or a cruel parody by Vladimir Nabokov, who was notorious in his ridicule of Freud – but who also said, "the spirit of parody always goes along with genuine poetry." Nonetheless, in spite of what may be of "art" here, I am troubled by what may amount to a lie in my late husband's professional misconduct as well as an abuse of the protocols of genres of presentation in these case studies. If only what imputes itself to be a narration of fabrication – a narration of a narration of fabrication – was only that. At the least, I can only hope and trust that what is given here is evidence of a sickness and that my husband was lying to *himself* as well as to us.

Introduction by the Editor
Stanley Pugh, PhD

Well-known psychologist Russell Clergy's usually affable but now distraught wife, Florence Wellington, entrusted me with the documents reproduced here out of a keen interest to protect her husband's clinical reputation. Sadly, this may not be possible. If Dr. Clergy discredited himself as a clinical theoretician with this set of falsified studies, he is nevertheless presented here in his own right as an exemplary case of a pseudologue – that is, a pathological liar. Ironically, the syndrome *pseudologia fantastica* was one of Russell Clergy's specialties. Perhaps, then, there is logic, however fantastic it is – a pseudo-logic one might say – to these "cases." We will attempt to discover whether this is true in order, at least, to establish a value otherwise for these "studies" and, thus, to rescue our subject from their falsifications: the purpose of publication here. If much of the current interest in pathological lying derives only from forensic psychiatrists in their assessment of defendants in legal cases, we, at least, have to put the discipline of our own house in order. In the texts that follow, I have therefore tried to identify within them what is fact and what is likely fiction.

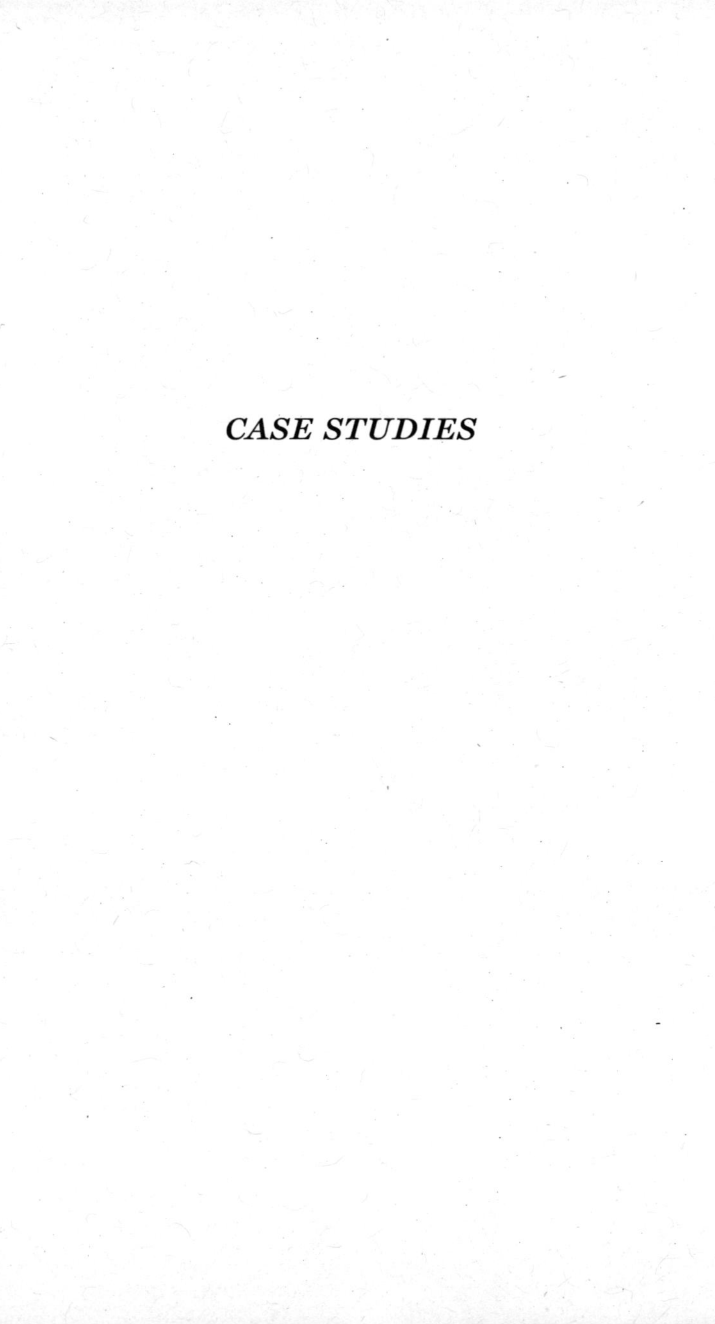

CASE STUDIES

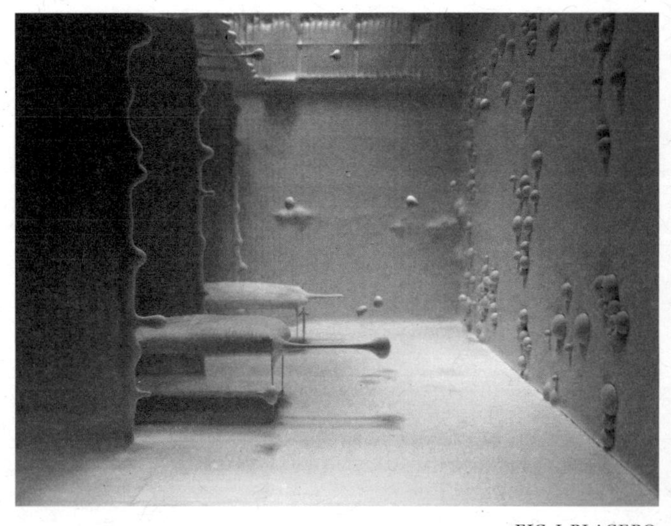

FIG. I PLACEBO

1. *Placebo*

The patient presented a number of delusions complaining that she was "slipping in and out of consciousness in shifts." She had a fantasy that she was in a pathological relationship with a man, a doctor – although perhaps it was the doctor who was pathological, if, indeed, he was a doctor. One day, mid-treatment, she came with a dream. She was in a hospital, in intensive care, having survived a car accident with her lover Jean, who was in a bed adjacent to her:

Here I am … lying next to my lover, Jean, in intensive care.
Slipping in and out of consciousness in shifts.
Life slowly dripping out of us.
Only a fifty percent chance of surviving our injuries …
a twenty five percent chance we will ever speak again.
We have been in a terrible car crash …
and were brought to the same hospital where he works as a surgeon.
Jean has been sleeping all of the time that I have been awake …
as he had been working the night shift.

PLACEBO

I try to leave messages for him through the nurses …
but they keep changing faces.
Too many drips to be changed and bloods to be drawn …
and while I have been lying here perfectly still, unable to move …
staring at the ceiling counting squares …
I have come to realize that I do not even know the person …
who I so badly want to survive.
As a mistress you fabricate the other persons life entirely in your imagination.
His descriptions have always been substitutes …
for the absence of shared experiences.
The married man, the caring father, the life saving doctor …
he seemed to think it necessary to portray himself as all of these.
Now he is muted he can no longer feed me this version of himself …
and the images I have constructed around his words are slowly disintegrating.
We met two years ago in the hospital where I worked as a nurse …
at the other side of town.
I would see him hurrying through the corridors … and developed a crush on him.
We spent hours chatting in the canteen until I was cautioned.
He never really seemed to have to go anywhere …
He never got beeped away …
I had heard of phantom doctors … roaming around hospitals.
Charming but unqualified men dressed in white coats.
Doing their imaginary rounds through endless corridors …
sporting a name-badge with a fancy title …
giving care behind cubicle curtains …
dispensing the treatments they in fact needed themselves.
I was in love and couldn't see that he was one of them.
Looking back of course the signs were obvious.
Although I used to see him coming out of the operating theatre …
with blood on his shoes …
he didn't really seem to know any of the other staff.
But before I had enough time to get suspicious …
he said he got a transfer to here.
This is the hospital he told me so much about …
although I was never allowed to visit him here.

PLACEBO

We would meet after work in my flat and he would tell me about different cases…
but his stories were getting less convincing …
details didn't match up.
When I confronted him with my suspicions …
That his medical knowledge was stolen from text books …
he suddenly claimed he was being sued for neglect.
One of the operations he was in charge of went wrong …
and a patient had died under his hands.
He seemed devastated and I really wanted to believe him.
Soon after he conveniently changed to the night shift.
Now we only overlapped for an hour each day.
He would visit me in the early mornings …
cleverly waking me precisely between two REM sequences …
when my brain was at its slowest.
Any questions I had left were silenced by his surgeon's fingers.
He would whisper things like he was the man I should continue mankind with.
I have tried to make it to his ward to find his name on a door.
Stumbling weekly across the hospitals white shiny veins …
I know I am walking around the backdrop against which his lies were set.
Because today all my suspicions have been confirmed …
For the first time I have managed to stay awake through the visiting hour …
nervous because just lying here in the same room seems like evidence.
I was perplexed to see his side of the family lounge remain empty.
No wife and kids have come to watch my lover sleep …
nor any cards or flowers from his colleagues.
It actually seems that none of the staff know him.
He couldn't be my husband …
but by being my lover he could hide his empty life.
When I asked him for the last time to leave his wife …
he panicked because he wasn't married.
He drove us into a tree …
hoping to take me with him to a place …
where I could receive his love …
without him having to be someone he wasn't.

At first, I thought, "the married man, the caring father, the life-saving doctor" – if only we could uncover the incidents in the past of the betrayal of her ego ideal that made her now so helpless.

Dissatisfied with my interpretation, the patient herself had done some research on *pseudologia fantastica* – not knowing it was already a specialty of mine – and had brought to light the striking case of Jean-Claude Romand, a Frenchman who in the early 1990s murdered his wife, children, and parents and attempted suicide when he feared exposure of his two decades of systematic lying. Whether his falsifications stemmed from his earlier claims to have passed a medical exam he did not sit or some other source, his story reveals the disproportionality inherent to this syndrome. He was not a doctor or medical researcher at all, although he claimed to work for the World Health Organization. Days he would wander the WHO offices, using their public services, fishing letterhead from wastebaskets, or doing his banking. On bogus business trips, he would travel to nearby Geneva and stay in an airport hotel, studying Swiss travel guides and medical journals, and buying toys for his children before departing for home. Daily life became an elaborate ruse that was threatened by slippage of the public realm into his private world. In the end, Romand was undone by a telephone call from his children's school to his office where, of course, no one had heard of him. The bubble of a self-sustained and self-contained world pricked and the ruse exposed, the climax to a seemingly routine life was disastrous. It seems our patient was disastrously tracing the dénouement to a similar case. Yet, the story presents a complicating twist to the usual situation of a man lying to his wife about his mistress. Here the man instead lies to his mistress about being married, which makes us wonder about the reality of this woman's story.

Pathological lying differs from confabulation, delusional thinking, factitious disorder, and malingering in the conscious or constructed aspect of its presentations. Our source here, Dike, Baranoski, and Griffith

(2005), somewhat awkwardly states, "While no consensus definition for pathological lying currently exists in the literature, the identified functional elements of the phenomena are: the repeated utterance of untruths; the lies are often repeated over a period of years, with the lies eventually becoming a lifestyle; material reward or social advantage does not appear to be a primary motivating force but the lying is an end in itself; an inner dynamic rather than an external reason drives the lies. But when an external reason is suspected, the lies are far in excess of the suspected internal reason; the lies are often woven into complex narratives." Yet *pseudologia fantastica* has an uncertain status as to whether it is a wilful act or a mental disorder. Consequently, it is not currently listed in the *Diagnostic and Statistical Manual of Mental Disorders* or in *The International Statistical Classification of Diseases and Related Health Problems*.

We wonder whether the satisfaction provided by this condition is in lying or in its fictional construction and ongoing performance. Whatever pathological lying is – wish psychosis, fantasy lies, or systematized delirium – it has a *fictional* character that is not simply lying. Indeed, quoting our source again, "it has also been suggested that the mental processes similar to those forming the basis of the impulse to literary creation in normal people is the foundation of the morbid romances and fantasies of those with *pseudologia fantastica.*" As in the constructions of fiction, this is "story telling that often has sort of a matrix of fantasy interwoven with some facts," a mixture, however, that must constantly be kept in balance even in face of the elaboration of new lies, for instance, those fabricated to prevent discovery. In our subject's case there was a necessary complementary construction paralleling her lover's lies. She said, "As a mistress you fabricate the person's life entirely in your imagination. His descriptions have always been substitutes for the absence of shared experience." But while her lover Jean further modified his lies to counter her suspicions, elaborating new scenarios in the process, the reverse was happening for her. "He would tell me about different cases. But his stories were getting less convincing. Details didn't match up." Now unconscious in the hospital, he could "no longer feed me this version of himself. And the images I have constructed around his words are slowly disintegrating."

Should we believe this patient? I have doubts. I wish I could consult this other doctor. Disintegrative personality disorder with attendant hallucinations would be my initial diagnosis, disregarding the patient's surmise of her lover's pathological lying. But before we had an opportunity to investigate the real source of these dissolving hallucinations, the patient stopped her visits. At this point in the analysis, I had begun to explain to her that I was still a writer but that now I was beginning to fear that part of me had become fiction. Perhaps it was my uncertainty about her treatment, or this statement itself, or her sense of *déjà vu* – before transference fully took – of the actions of her lover Jean reflected in my own that caused the patient to break off her sessions.

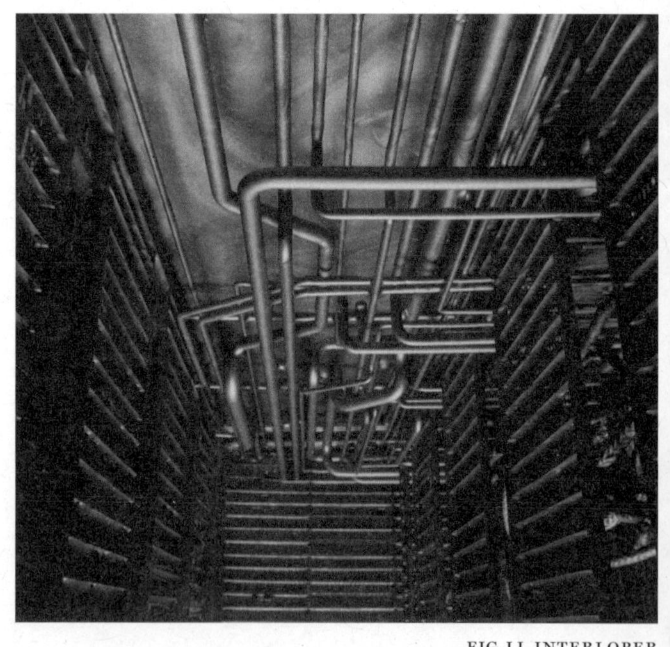

FIG. I I INTERLOPER

2. *Interloper*

[EDITOR'S NOTE: No notes or case study exist for *Interloper*, only what I am calling here a "script" similar in structure to the "dream" told in *Placebo*. Internal evidence suggests that *Interloper* is related to *Placebo* although, of course, details and tone vary. The two seem vaguely to signal to each other from two distinct universes, yet they wind the same Möbius strip of hospital corridors. Out of sync in the first, the two characters or patients temporarily knot together at the end of the second.

Interloper now is told from a man's point of view, but this point of view is severely divided. A near death experience has split the man's consciousness and while his body habitually follows routine, plying his fallacious trade as a medical practitioner in the same hospital in which he is now a patient, his thoughts float above, pulled like a balloon, surveying this disconcerting disjunction. Returning from his rounds to the room were he had awakened earlier, he mechanically performs a procedure: cutting, not the silvery cord connecting his mind and body, but the umbilical cord of a baby with a head like his own. This act reattaches him both to his own body and to his delusion of being a doctor. "Feeling my hands mechanically carry out the procedure, I hear myself say routinely: 'Here you are madam, a nice tidy knot for the belly button of your little man.'" Clearly, the mother is the deceived woman from *Placebo* but now strangely pregnant and delivering a child.

Here follows the script, whose status I keep in reserve.]

A question occurred to me while I slept …
And I awake to find myself out of bed … floating up to the ceiling.
I look down … surprised to see my body still lying in a hospital bed.
I heard about this … a near death experience … No need to panic …
Although looking down again I see my dormant self …
has also escaped from the ever-increasing dosages of drugs …
the nurses administer and is now leaving the room dressed in a doctor's coat.
I am slowly pulled along following myself …

INTERLOPER

Holding together the compromising folds of my hospital gown.
As I float along the ceiling low enough to hear myself …
softly repeat a private little mantra …
"Nothing is a more powerful placebo than the word …
As the organisms of diseases are naked to the human eye anyway."
Waking up after being in a nine month coma …
must have tricked the brain …
As I seem to think I am a doctor.
I take a scalpel out of my pocket …
and we stumble through double doors into an operating theatre.
Here a matronly nurse washes our hands … ·
and I nauseously get to witness myself perform a caesarean …
While I get a peck on the check by the patients floating other half,
she whispers … "I have seen you around …
You used to sit in the waiting room with a notepad …
When did you become a doctor?"
I explain to her that I am still a writer but now …
I am beginning to fear that part of me has become fiction.
Below I hear myself announce to the team of surgeons …
"I'll be back shortly … I really have to phone my wife now"
I leave the operating theatre …
and start ranting endlessly into a pay phone in the corridor.
Undisturbed by the fact that my words seem to be falling silent …
against the clicking of the dial tone.
I am interrupted when an elderly lady taps me on the shoulder.
She is convinced that someone is playing Vera Lynn records loudly …
somewhere in the building …
and the sound is exiting through the radiator pipes that end in her room.
"I have a very tight schedule but I'll see what I can do" …
I hear myself say.
We then proceed to the basement …
a mute underworld of biotechnology laboratories.
Air-conditioning hums softly …
and rows of padded cells acoustically absorb the shrieking of brainless birds.
Tanks full of frogs waiting to be observed under fabricated foliage …

while curiously studying their own reflections infinitely repeated in the glass.
I start stacking the tanks carefully on a trolley …
and ride them out into the hospital garden.
"Don't you all know frogs need moonlight to conceive?"
I shout to no one in particular …
Ladies of the night shift begin gathering around …
All greeting me with a rehearsed regularity.
"Should you be doing this so soon after your accident?" …
one of them asks while the rest fondly peer into the tanks.
I hear my name being called out …
and I turn around to see an elderly lady in a lab coat approach.
I remember her from a long time ago …
"What a surprise that you have come back to visit us," she says …
"Most of them never do and I don't blame them.
Our program was a cruel experiment …
Hopefulbut naïve parents gave their children away …
To this so-called factory for budding geniuses.
A nursery with plain grey walls …
and only a few toys to play with.
To keep the signal to noise ratio low.
And to protect the growing prodigies from an overload of unnecessary information,
especially nature, they were never let out of the basement.
Until the hospital became their parent and they ignored their own."
I want to hear more but am briskly pulled away …
by my pilot who is sweating profusely in his hurry through the building.
When we enter the room we woke up in earlier …
there is a woman lying in a bed on the other side of the curtain …
I hadn't noticed before.
She speaks to me softly, her eyes resting on a spot exactly between my two selves …
as if there lies the truth.
She is awkwardly holding a pair of surgical scissors to her chest …
and I hover closer hoping that she can cut the silver cord …
that will separate me from my confused self.
But suddenly she closes her eyes and opens her mouth …
stirred by a sharp pain.

After what seems like ages of me helplessly watching her suffer …
she reaches under the blankets and holds up a little baby boy.
It's wrinkled little head resembling my own.
I have to do something …
I slide down, adjusting back into the man …
I have had the short privilege not to be …
and feel my brain fill again with nonsense again.
She hands me the scissors …
I close my eyes avoiding the sight of blood.
Feeling my hands mechanically carry out the procedure …
I hear myself say routinely;
"Here you are madam … a nice tidy knot for the belly button of your little man."

[EDITOR'S NOTE: At first I wondered whether *Interloper* might be a case of "double consciousness," a theory proposed by Wendt for pathological lying in his 1911 "Ein Beitrag zur Kasuistik der Pseudologia phantastica," in which (according to Dike, Baranoski, and Griffith) "two forms of life run side by side, the actual and desired, and the desired becomes preponderant and decisive." Consciousness hovering above the body, as in this case, is an apt metaphor for this syndrome. (The founder of the science of neurology, Hughlings Jackson, wrote of this phenomenon of "doubling of consciousness" in 1880: "There is (1) the quasi-parasitical state of consciousness (dreamy state), and (2) there are remains of normal consciousness and, thus, there is double consciousness ... a mental diplopia.") Then because of the similarity of the two stories, *Placebo* and *Interloper*, I thought that perhaps here might be a rare case of pseudology *à deux*, that is, a shared pseudology, which is considered a variant of *folie à deux*, with pathological lying now replacing psychosis. I soon rejected this idea since the distress of the first case does not match what I can't help but think of as the cavalier quality of the second. The divided point of view, however, suggests a subject at war with itself, part of the psyche protesting to the lies and deceptions of its doppelgänger.

Finally, I began to consider the uncomfortable thought that Clergy might have fabricated this dream-story on the model of what his patient brought to his previous case (*Placebo*). To what end, though? Why was he inhabiting the character of a pseudologue: to empathize with a victim in order to understand the syndrome? Or was this merely a genre exercise, simulating the patient's dream of *Placebo* but from the other side, that is, from the point of view of the pseudologue? One non-clinical definition of pseudology I have found talks of it as "the act of lying, especially when humorously proposed as an art or system." This would explain a fictional exercise, if only it were that. So would pseudology as a pretended field of study, if the pretended field of study itself is invented – as for instance in the many fabulations of the Museum of Jurassic Technology in Los Angeles. (Jacques Derrida points out the intertwined problems in defining the pseudological in that "lying, deceiving, and being mistaken are all three included in the category of the pseudological. In Greek, *pseudos* can mean lie as well as falsehood, cunning, or mistake, and deception or fraud, as well as poetic invention, which increases the possible misunderstandings about what a misunderstanding may mean.") Most worrisome would be if this script were an outright lie: a fabrication masquerading as an actual case study that Clergy intended to publish (as in the literary forgeries, the *Hitler Diaries* and *Autobiography of Howard Hughes*, for instance) but which his death cut short. Such an exercise raises the crucial question: Do pseudologues know they are lying?

An expert who knows the symptoms and all the tricks of resistance would be a formidable fabricator. The humour throughout, the recalcitrant return to and acceptance of the pathology at the conclusion of the script, both make me think perhaps that Clergy is playing with us. His superiority, thinking he could get away with this deception in the case at hand, would answer in the affirmative to my earlier question. Yes, I believe he knew he was lying!]

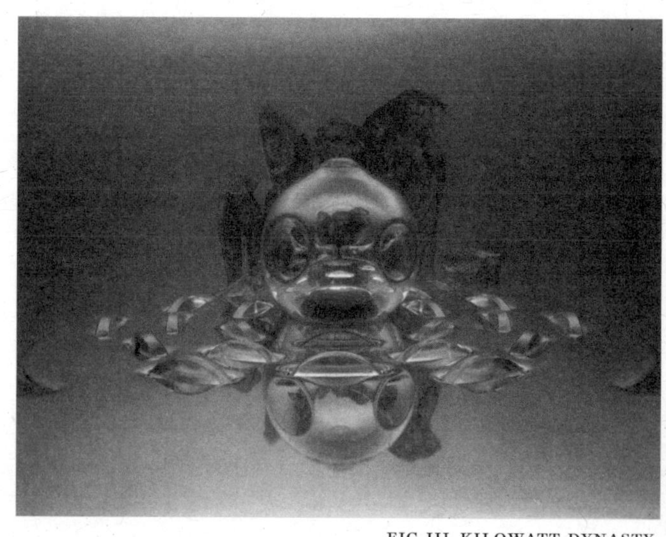

FIG. III KILOWATT DYNASTY

40

3. *Kilowatt Dynasty*

[EDITOR'S NOTE: We are on no less certain ground in the case entitled *Kilowatt Dynasty*. That is to say, temporally and spatially as well. Whatever its status, the case introduces a new syndrome: the Inverted Dream syndrome. I say introduces. I might just as well have said *invented*. More importantly, though, the analysis veers towards neurology, before rejecting it, in that it begins to map out a mental landscape that, in fact, has accompanied the scenarios of all these cases but has remained unstated. "Unstated," because of the prejudice towards conceptual schemata and language disorders in analysis (whether psychiatric, psychoanalytic, or neurological), even when applied to vision. Macrae (as reported by Oliver Sacks) agrees here with me when he "finds the explanation of defective schemata, or defective visual processing and integration, inadequate." It's an old rivalry between the left and right brain and their respective advocates. But back to Clergy...]

The central question, or speculation, of this case is the double reversion: firstly, the question why the patient's mother freely returned to become captive in a hostage taking, falling victim to what has been called the Stockholm syndrome; secondly, whether the first syndrome is only a screen for the second – what I call, following what is revealed in this analysis, the "Inverted Dream syndrome." In the end, inversion rather than reversion is the figure of this story. It is question not of *why* but *where* all this takes place.

First the story that the patient presented to me:

Let's try to imagine that I am going to be born in 17 years.
Let's, in our heads, go forward to the year 2016
The year in which I will be conceived by the country's most famous hidden couple.
The year the worlds largest Dam … The Three Gorges Dam …
will have just been built in our province.
The year one million people will be relocated to prefab towns …

KILOWATT DYNASTY

for the creation of the large water reservoir.
And the year …
the notorious TV program Kilowatt Dynasty will be on.
This tele-shopping program will be broadcast from a flashy underwater centre …
at the bottom of the newly formed lake.
The country's biggest multinational, selling electrical appliances
will expect a big shopping craze and finance the program as a marketing tool.
People will still be able to watch their old valley …
while being seduced into buying a washing machine.
And no one other than my mother …
will get the privileged job of presenting it.
A divorced mother-of-one-ex-quiz-show-host …
then in her late thirties …
will give it her best in a tangy coloured two-piece …
leaning casually on shiny washing machines …
in front of various underwater scenes.
But in the third month the slick backdrops will change due to heavy siltation.
What happens next depends on who you'll speak to.
The man who is going to make a difference in her life …
is then still slumped in front of the television in his new living room.
My future father is neither here nor there.
During the construction of the dam …
he will have handcuffed himself to the fence around the visitors centre.
While activists chained elsewhere will be locked up …
he will have luckily put himself in a place …
where a lot of national and international camera crews will film him …
so he won't be arrested.
Now he will be disrespected in the activists' hidden scene
and having nothing on his cv …
other than handcuffing himself to a fence …
will have made him a lonely man.
While irregularities rush through his mind …
he thinks of a way of reinstating his activist grace.
In the night of October the 18 he goes up to the centre …
walks past the sleeping guard …

comes live on air and makes an announcement …
That he has taken mum hostage.
He makes no clear demands but is armed.
This will be bad news …
bad news for him …
because mum won't actually be in the centre when this happens.
She would have been seen by several witnesses going around the new town above.
So just as the word will spread about her apparent escape …
her head will appear on the program's last ever broadcast …
in which she just repeats his exact words.
The fact that she will have re-entered the centre voluntarily …
without telling anyone of her decision …
and leaving her teenage son above water …
will have everyone looking frantically for an explanation.
Each member of our small family will have their own theories …
involving her quest for love, fame or just adventure.
But I think that she will have started suffering from ..:
"The Inverted Dream syndrome" …
which is dangerously common to astronauts …
when the spaces and events in their dreams will look more real …
than the everyday dark nothingness of outer space.
Until they are convinced that they are awake …
while dreaming of their wives in bungalows back on earth …
and that their empty floaty reality is actually a dream.
Mum will start believing …
she dreams of being in a transparent building underwater …
surrounded by an oddly familiar landscape …
while wearing an orange uniform … and flesh coloured tights
and these people she doesn't know, but know her …
keep ringing her about washing machines.
And when she thinks she is awake …
she sleepwalks out of the centre into the lift …
which takes her up to the new town above.
Here she'll wander around aimlessly …
looking absent

not speaking to anyone
Just like on the afternoon father thinks he takes her hostage …
she will be hovering around town.
While dreaming of getting tired …
she will unknowingly return to the centre
… to go to sleep.

It is hard to know which inversion is the most fantastic: the event taking place seventeen years in the future when the narrator will be born; the underwater life; or the substitution of waking and dreaming. Since the first two inversions are pre-given in the story, the crux seems to be the submission: Did the mother wish her captivity? In the Stockholm syndrome, captives unexpectedly express loyalty to their abductors. The most celebrated recent case is that of socialite Patty Hearst (a.k.a., Tania), abducted by and then an accomplice to the robberies of the Symbionese Liberation Army in 1974–75. But here, the narrator speculates that her future mother in actuality was a victim, instead, of the "Inverted Dream syndrome," where dream events seem more real than ordinary waking life. She was submitting, her mother believed, only to her sleep patterns, while in reality she was returning from her sleepwalking to her working life. Her submission to captivity was an accident of her hallucinated reality, or, rather, unreality. However, what I mean by wish is the desire for this unreality, even if not consciously thought.

Such states of experiential hallucination are common in epileptic seizures. Wilder Penfield had simulated these experiences in the operating room and reported them in his monumental study "The Brain's Record of Auditory and Visual Experience," published in *Brain* (1963) where he wrote, "Rodin *et al.* (1955) believe that the experiential hallucinations in seizure patterns are closely connected with the patient's wishes, anxieties or neurotic conflicts, even when the patient had a temporal lobe neoplasm," but Penfield himself concluded otherwise. Sacks notes, "Such epileptic hallucinations or dreams, Penfield showed, are never phantasies: they are always memories, and memories of the most precise and vivid kind, accompanied by the emotions which accompanied the original experience." (Again, as Sacks points out, this is another variety of Jacksonian mental diplopia or double consciousness, which we, as well, have found in other cases.) The mother could not wish such a return: Our floaty subject was returning only to her amnesiac state produced by routine, not fantasy – a routine carried out, however, in a fantastic locale.

[EDITOR'S NOTE: A similar case exists in fragments in Clergy's notes, identified as *Day-Glo*, in which a woman irrevocably retreated to a virtual reality theme park (developed by her husband from an unsuccessful greenhouse agro-business), having fallen in love there with an earlier version of her husband.]

If these fantasies are memories, they are those instead of our pre-foetal narrator: memories in advance – that is to say, those of the future. The floating world is as much her own as that of her mother's. The artificially induced memories that Penfield explored, therefore, are not distorted as those we come across in *our* clinical practice, the best evidence of which – what is inaccessible to us otherwise – is found in images fabricated by artists. Another author, reviewing the case history of Winchester Repeating Rifle heiress Sarah Winchester, has written about a similar madness of the image that appears to be internally produced. Philip Monk perceptively writes, "As individual subjects who constitute ourselves through self-certitude, we need to think that perception is something *we* possess, knowing, in spite of virtual fusion, that *our* perception and *that* reality are united momentarily in *this* image. Could we imagine that perception might be split otherwise, that it might be internally *other*, belonging not to us but to a doppelgänger to whom we belong? From our *perspective*, we set an image at a distance *outside* us, protecting ourselves by guarding this fragile divide of 'outside' us, so how could we be receptive to possession?" The memories of the floating world of our subject, however, are more benign. Indeed, there is a comfort in delusion, as if the divisions between inner and outer, reality and fiction, truth and lies do not, in the end, really count.

[EDITOR'S NOTE: This last text by Clergy seems to be a plea as much as a case study. This doctor sleepwalked out of his existence – certainly, out of his professional reputation.]

**Saskia Olde Wolbers' works
cited in *Case Studies***

Kilowatt Dynasty (2000), 6 min DV
Voice-over: Jean Lee

Placebo (2002), 6 min DV
Voice-over: Sukie Smith

Interloper (2003), 6 min DV
Voice-over: Ian Michie
Sounds: Jem Finer

Part 2

Postscript to a Fiction
Philip Monk

Postscript to a Fiction

Philip Monk

Whatever there is of fiction here surely must end.
Yet, Saskia Olde Wolbers' works proceed by fiction.
Hence, the nature of the preceding exercise, preface
to this postscript, which now, really (I promise), will
deal with the works in the exhibition – *Trailer* (2005)
and *Deadline* (2007). The former exercise proceeded
by example not explanation: by the example of Olde
Wolbers' fictions, but also by the example of genre,
by means of genres of fiction, which should have
been obvious to the reader. Olde Wolbers' scripts
join fictional and documentary elements. In a lecture,
the artist has said that her videos "are often loosely
based on real life events from newspapers and television, stories that fascinate often because of the lack
of insight into the situation described."

Likewise, my text made itself from a concatenation
of elements that are real and fictional: using Olde
Wolbers' research sources, that is to say, the *real*
(the pathology *pseudologia fantastica*, the actual
story of Jean-Claude Romand, and Olde Wolbers'
interest in the case studies of neurologist Oliver
Sacks, for instance), but employing them at an
interpretative remove, through genres of fictions –
here predominantly that of case studies, which are,

again, framed within literary devices. (Philip Monk is not the author, other characters are; and the "case studies" are only shorthand to touch upon subjects in the videos; hence, treating the scripts and artworks as if they were the patient's talk or dreams, indeed the patient him- or herself, who, of course, is other than the artist.) This device was a way of talking about fiction through fiction because Saskia Olde Wolbers' work, to a large part, is not only fictional but is about the making of fictions.

What is obvious, however, is not necessarily said. If the said corresponds to content, the unsaid corresponds to the determining genre. (Of course, the unsaid exists as well on the level of the text, as its unconscious, so to speak.) But Olde Wolbers not only joins fictional and documentary elements in her scripts, she links them to series of images, themselves fabricated and quite fantastic in their nature.[1] The said and unsaid, however, do not now correspond to word and image respectively. This would only repeat the prejudice hinted above that we witness in neurology – where language schemata and their aphasic disruptions have oriented neurological studies to fixate on the left brain.* Instead, as Michel Foucault has written in *The Birth of the Clinic: An Archaeology of Medical Perception*, "We must re-examine the

---

* *"One important reason for the neglect of the right, or 'minor', hemisphere, as it has always been called, is that while it is easy to demonstrate the effects of variously located lesions on the left side, the corresponding syndromes of the right hemisphere are much less distinct. It is presumed, usually contemptuously, to be more 'primitive' than the left, the latter being seen as the unique flower of human evolution…. On the other hand, it is the right hemisphere which controls the crucial powers of recognising reality which every living creature must have in order to survive. The left hemisphere, like a computer tacked onto the basic creatural brain, is designed for programs and schematics; and classical neurology was more concerned with schematics than with*

original distribution of the visible and invisible insofar as it is linked with the division between what is stated and what remains unsaid.... We must place ourselves, and remain once and for all, at the level of the fundamental *spatialization* and *verbalization* of the pathological." Saskia Olde Wolbers' video works employ a unique way of entwining this inseparable spatialization and verbalization of the pathological.

Nonetheless, we are always prejudiced towards language, no less so in the case of these videos where we are led by the script's narrative as if in explanation or assurance that the strange tale has a meaning. The narrative, however, also leads us through a corresponding space that is not as assured in its coordinates. (Narrative expectation corresponds to classical geometry, but as Foucault writes, "Every great thought in the field of pathology lays down a configuration for disease whose spatial requisites are not necessarily those of classical geometry.") That is, the space corresponds to the narrative flow but is not its illustration; rather it is a correlate of the mental state of the narrator or subject – less a container than a Möbius strip that entwines language and space. The two – narrative and space – cannot be separated, just as the floating movement through the liquid environment is one with its scene. The environment itself dissolves, drips, and melts

---

reality, so that when, at last, some of the right-hemisphere syndromes emerged, they were considered bizarre....

"Inner difficulties and outer difficulties match each other here. It is not only difficult, it is impossible, for patients with certain right-hemisphere syndromes to know their own problems – a peculiar and specific 'anosagnosia', as Babinski called it. And it is singularly difficult, for even the most sensitive observer, to picture the inner state, the 'situation', of such patients, for this is almost unimaginatively remote from anything he himself has ever known. Left-hemisphere syndromes, by contrast, are relatively easily imagined." Oliver Sacks, "Preface," The Man Who Mistook His Wife for a Hat.)

as the scene separates from itself and fuses differently. The eye of the camera establishes a disembodied movement that is unvaryingly sustained even through edits, producing a continuous hallucinated or dream-like state. This confusion of environment *is* the confusion of waking and dreaming of the woman in *Kilowatt Dynasty*, with the motion of the image her sleepwalking reversal: "their empty floaty reality is actually a dream." Similarly, the movement in *Interloper* replicates the dissociated "floating up to the ceiling" of its "confused self" as we follow the narrator's unseen double through the hospital corridors. Or, likewise, it reflects the narrator of *Placebo* "perfectly still" in her bed yet "slipping in and out of consciousness in shifts." Her scene dissolves along with the fabrications that supported her lover's lies. (Fabrications are both his *and* her own: "as a mistress you fabricate the other person's life entirely in your imagination.") In the "background against which his lies were set," the hospital he told her so much about, "details didn't match up," and she finds now that "the images I have constructed around his words are slowly disintegrating."

Contrary to images, would words be exempt from similar disintegration? Between words and images, there would be no place for the truth. "She speaks to me softly," says *Interloper*'s narrator, "her eyes resting on a spot exactly between my two selves as if there lies the truth." Truth cannot be spatialized, indeed stabilized, in what is already dissociated. No more should we attempt, therefore, to find any truth between the two levels of the artwork, that is, as a presumed unity of language and image. A lie, rather than the truth, is the starting point.

Trailer

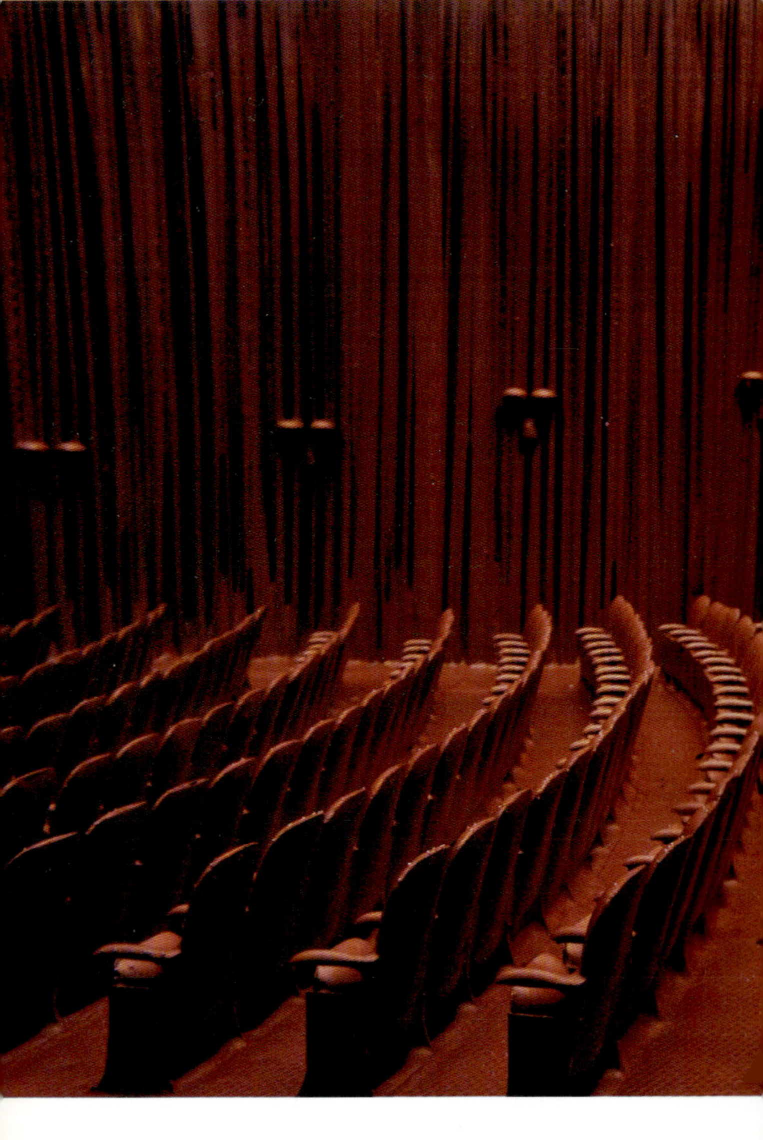

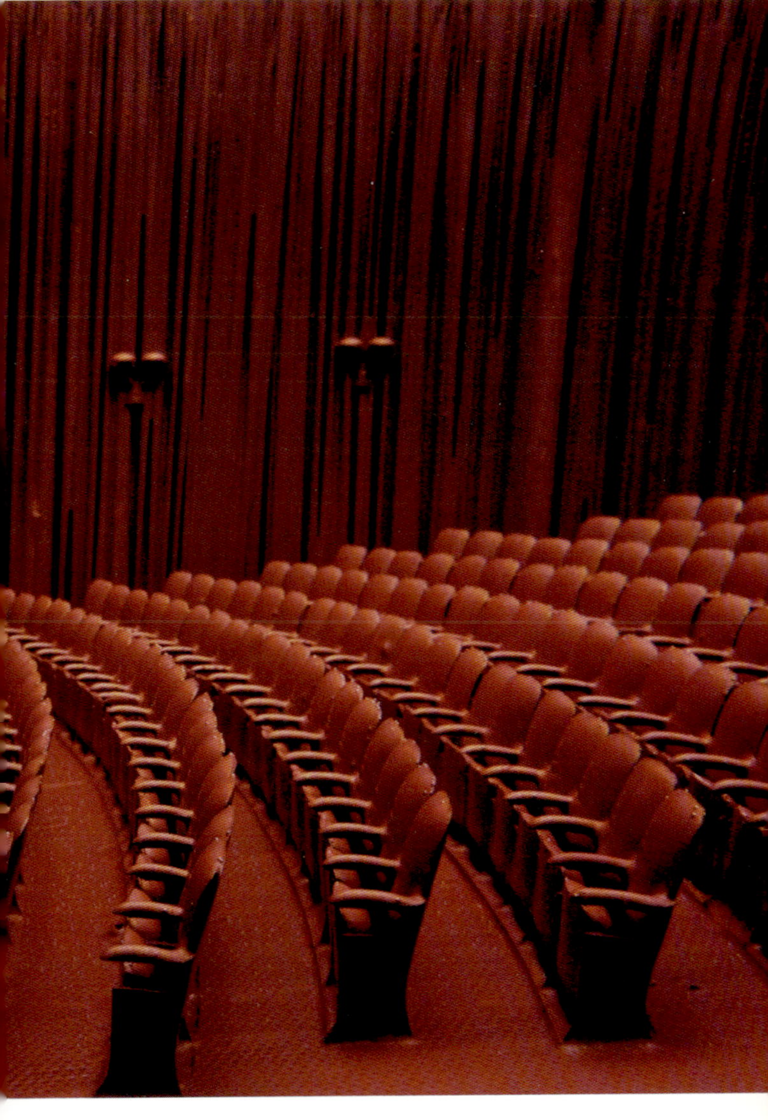

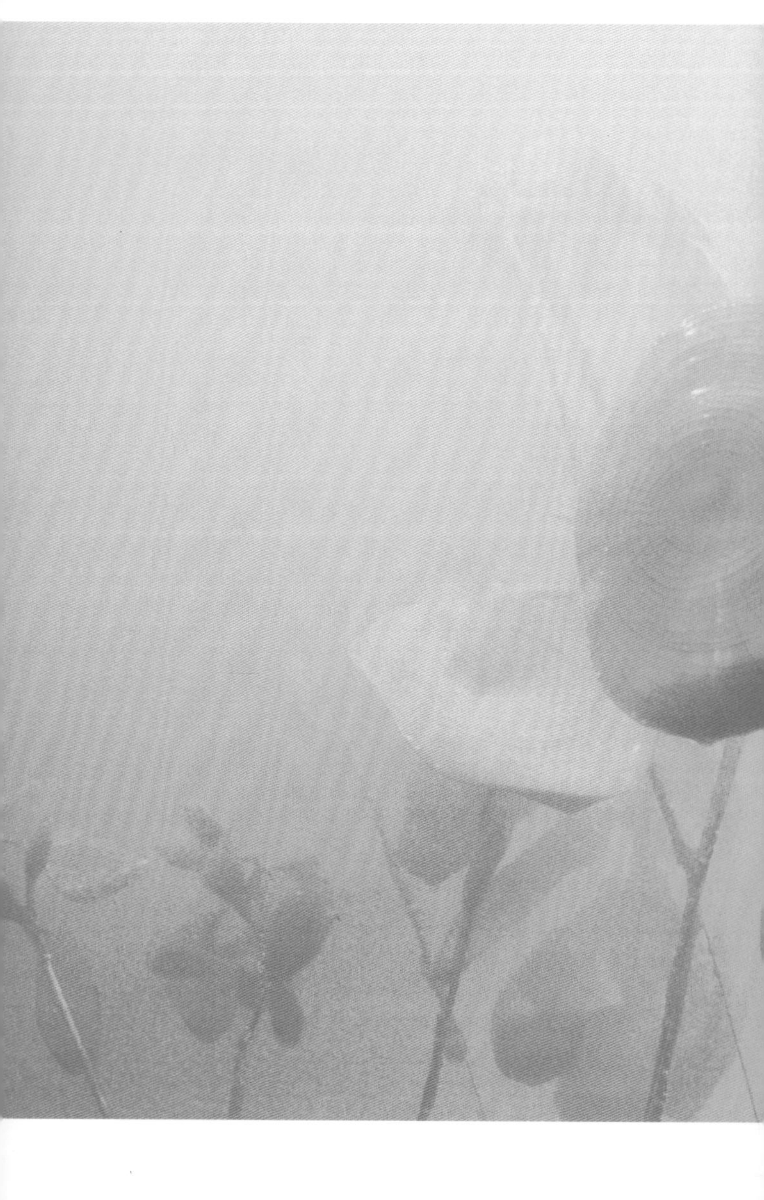

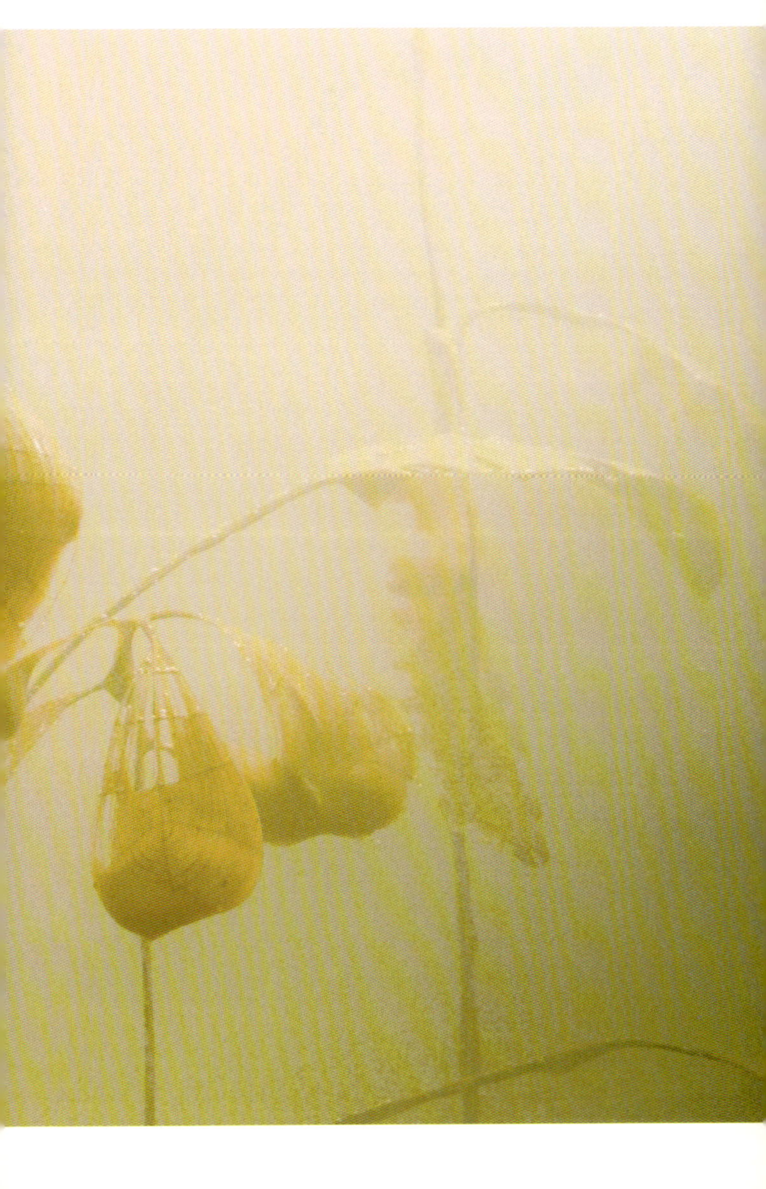

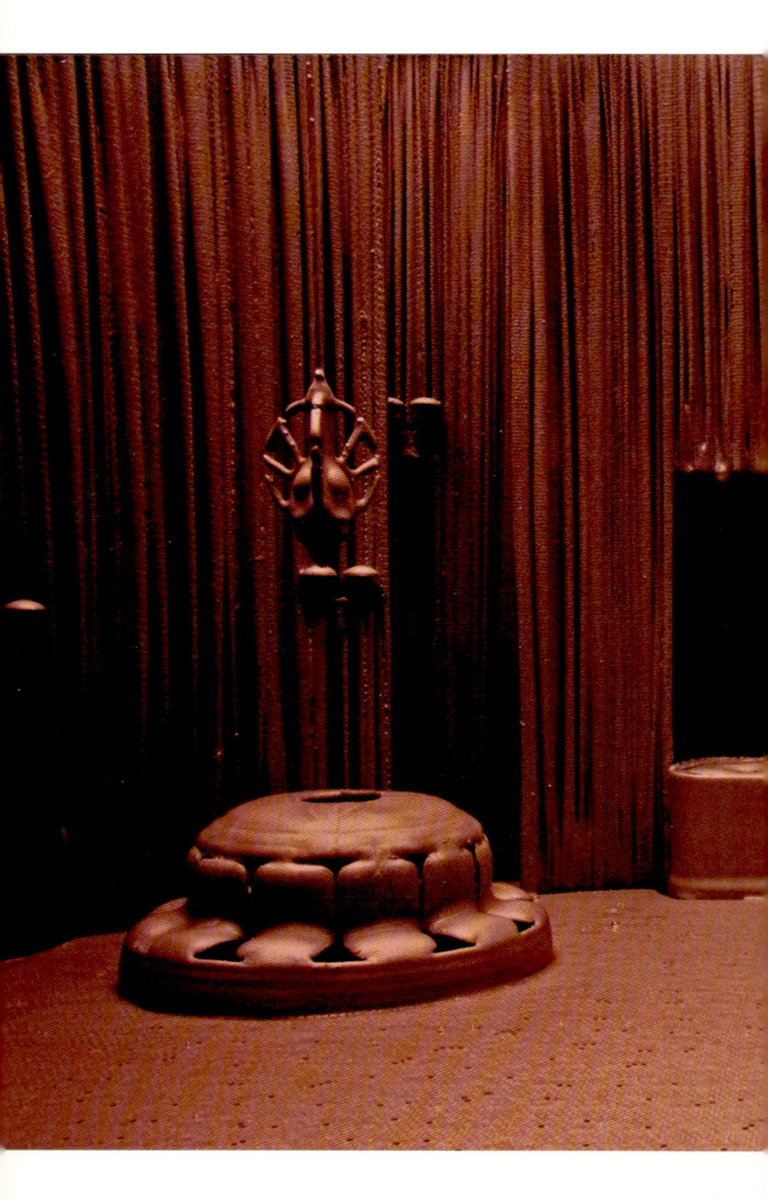

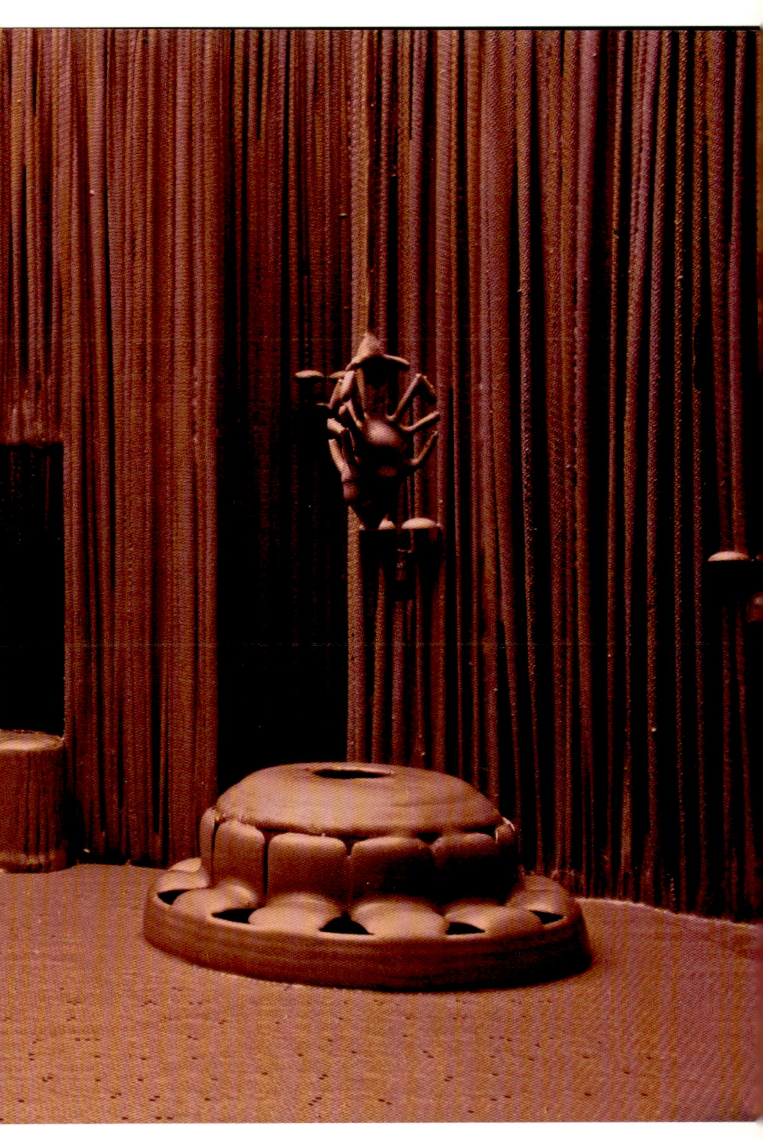

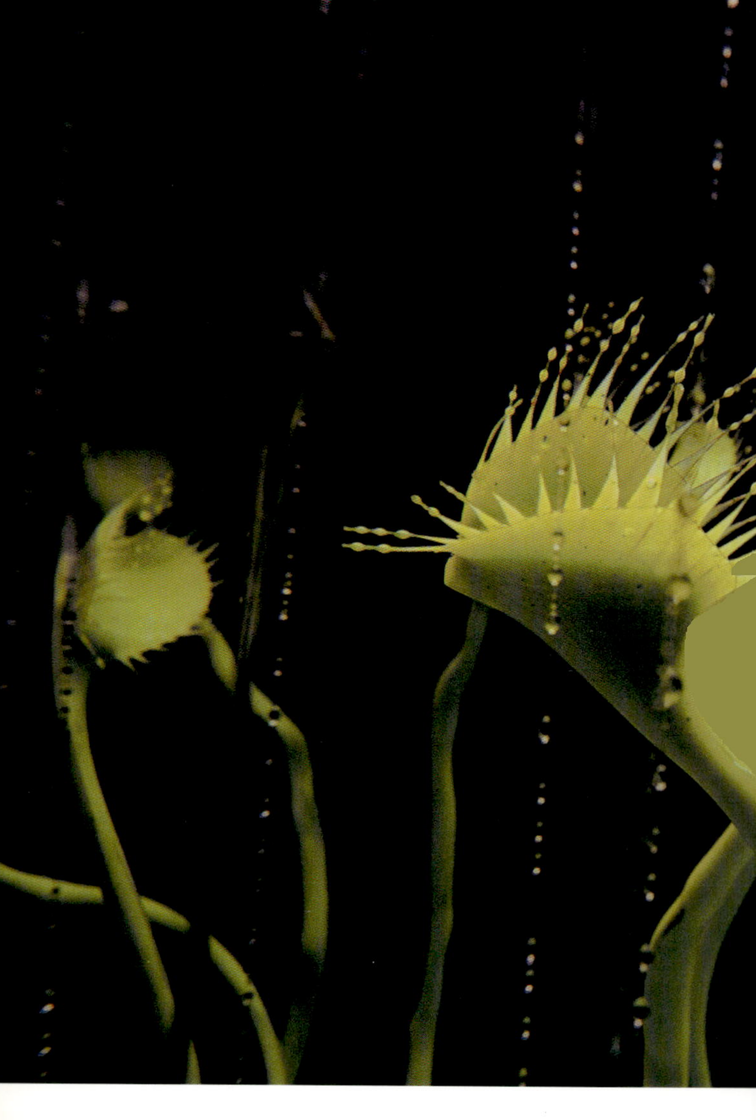

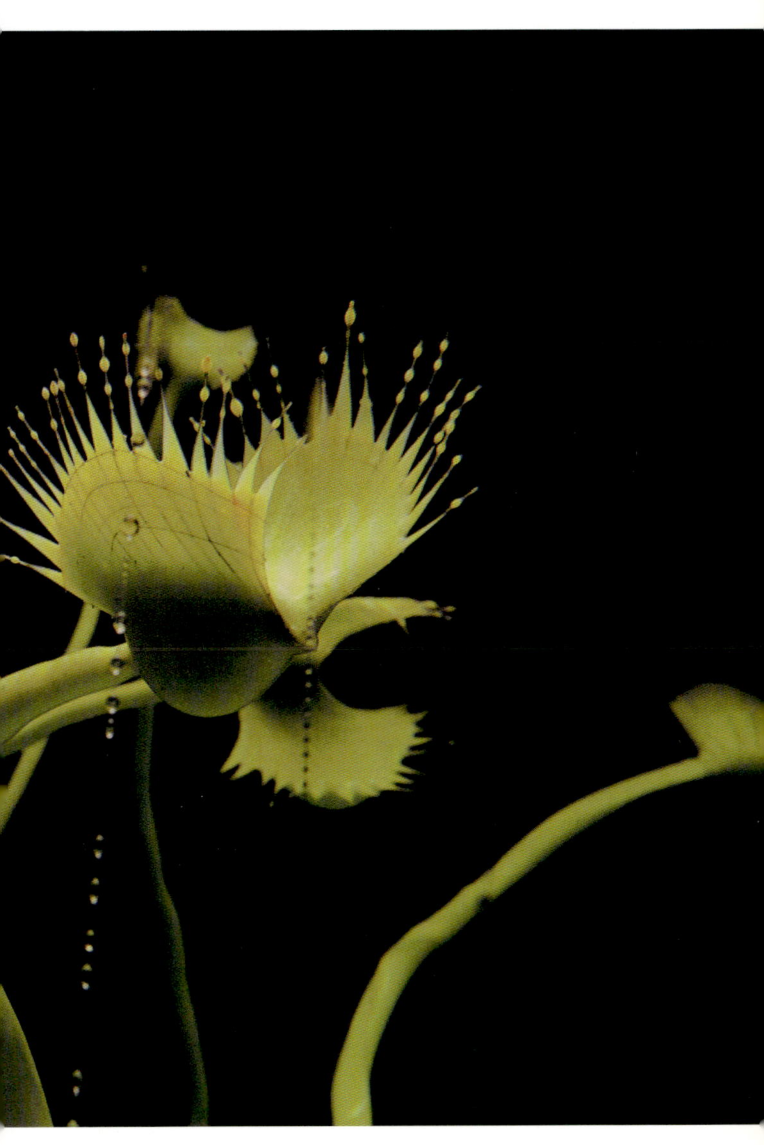

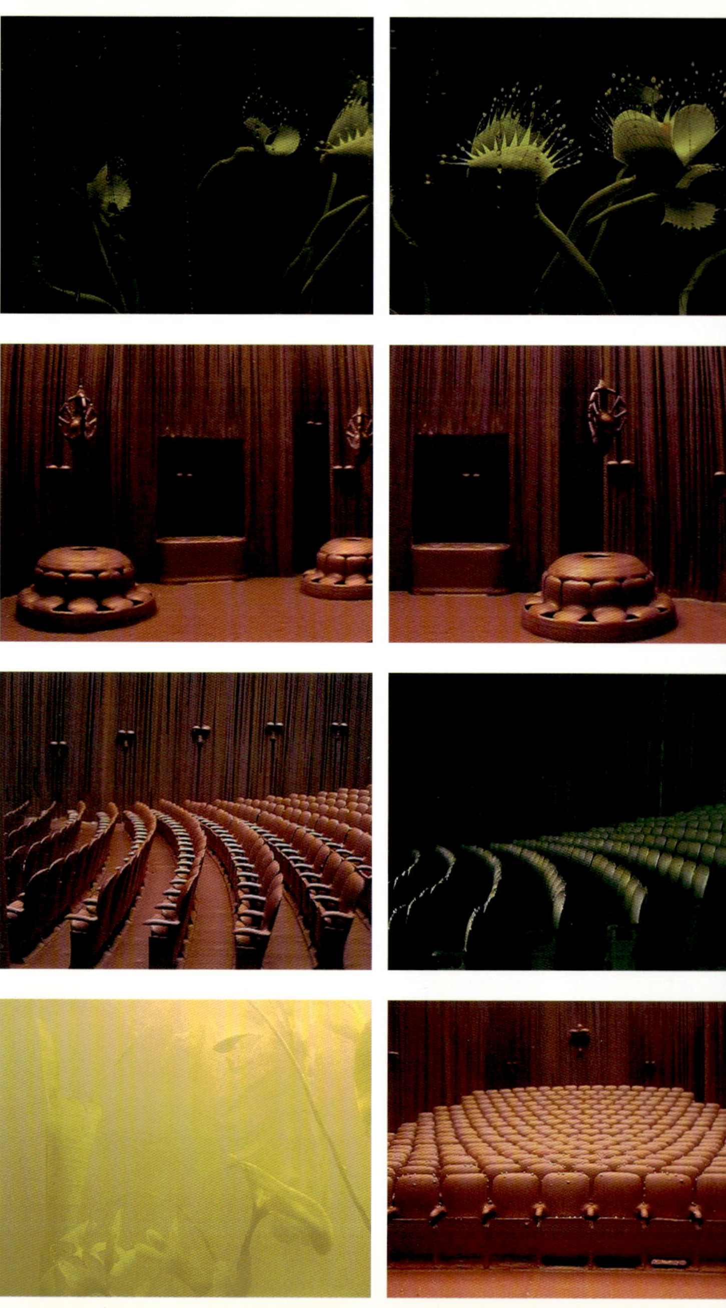

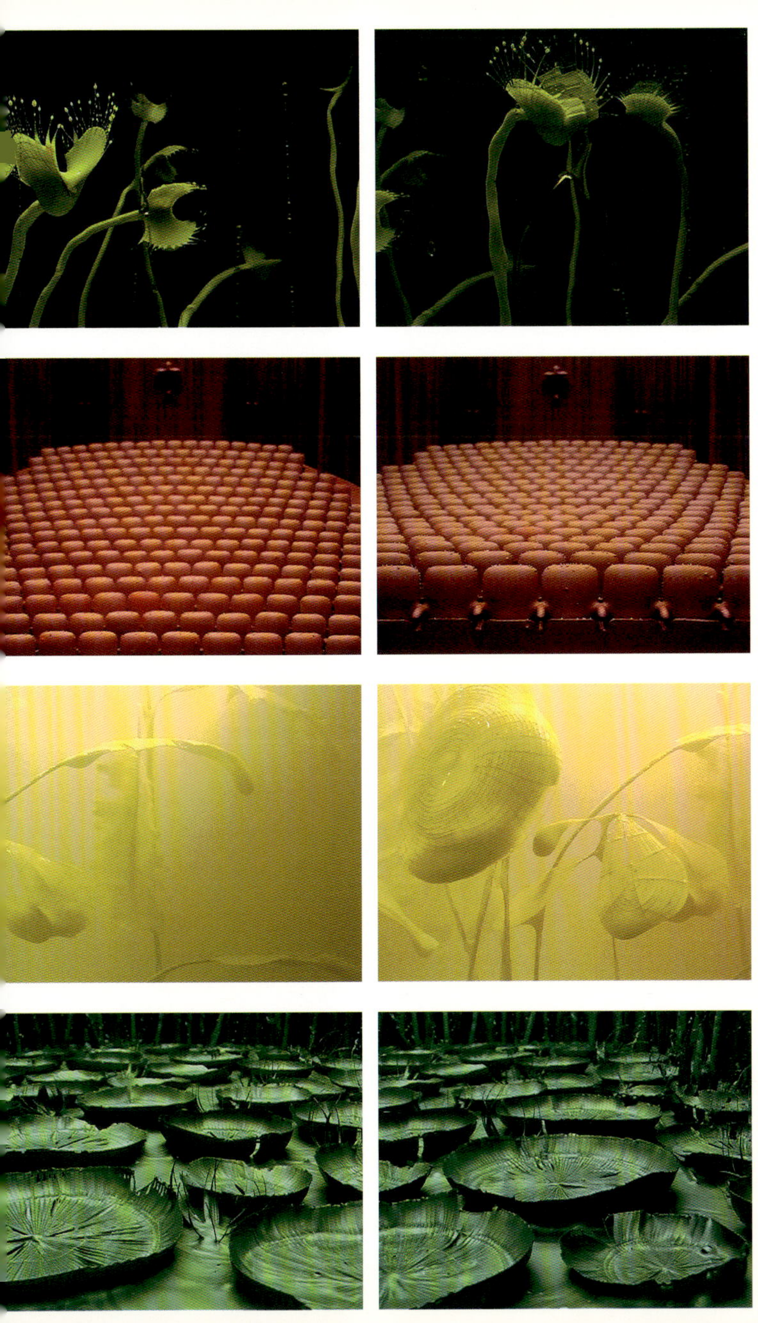

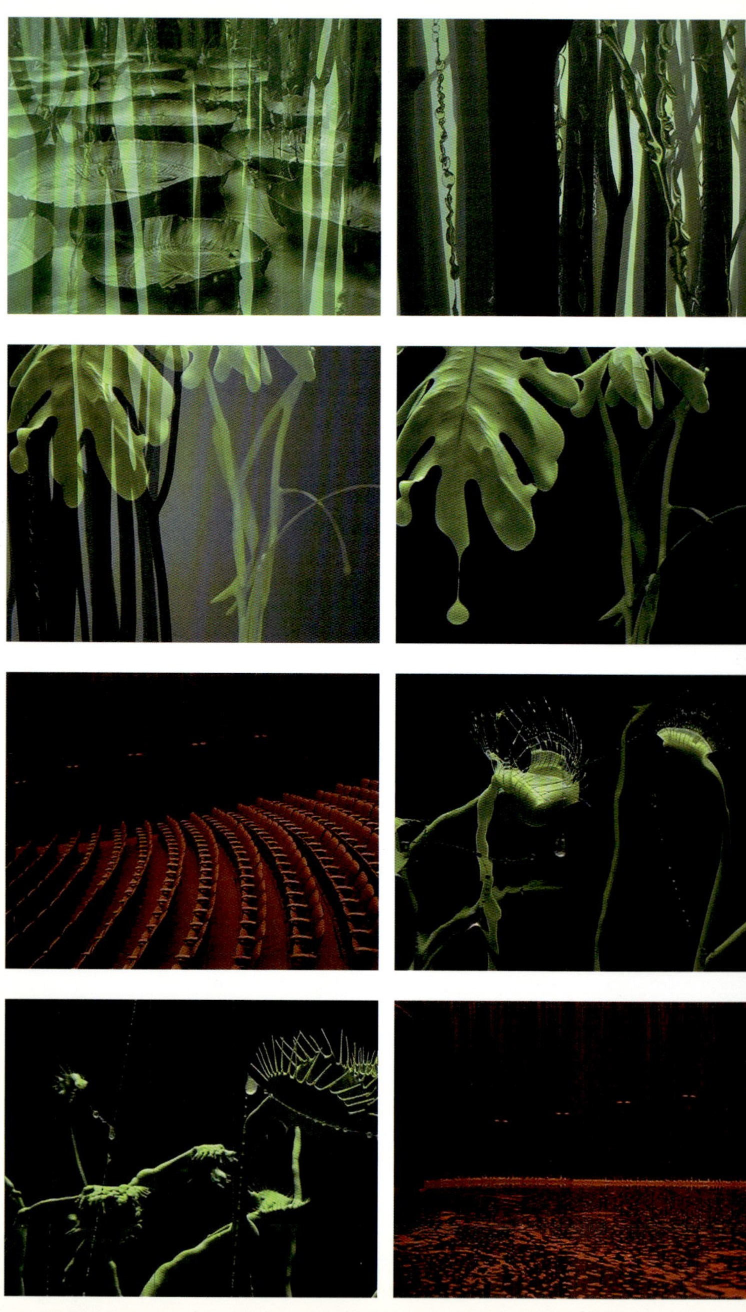

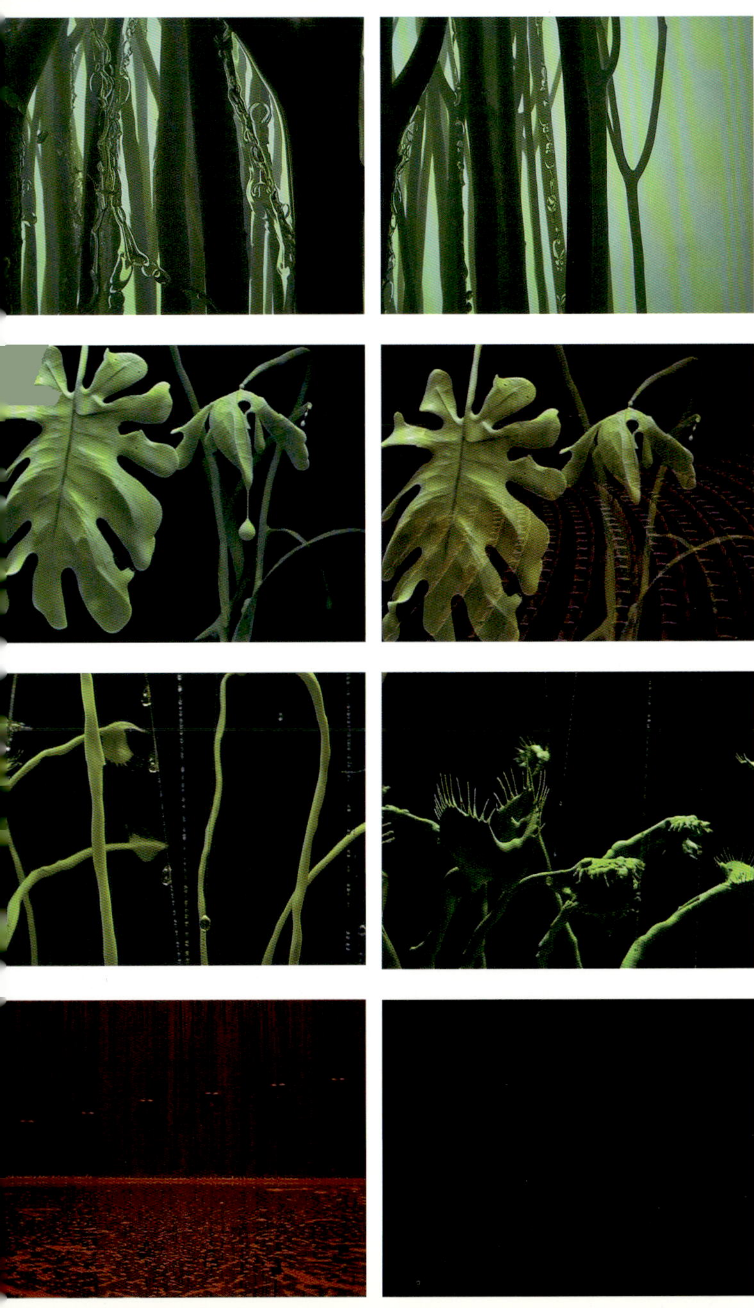

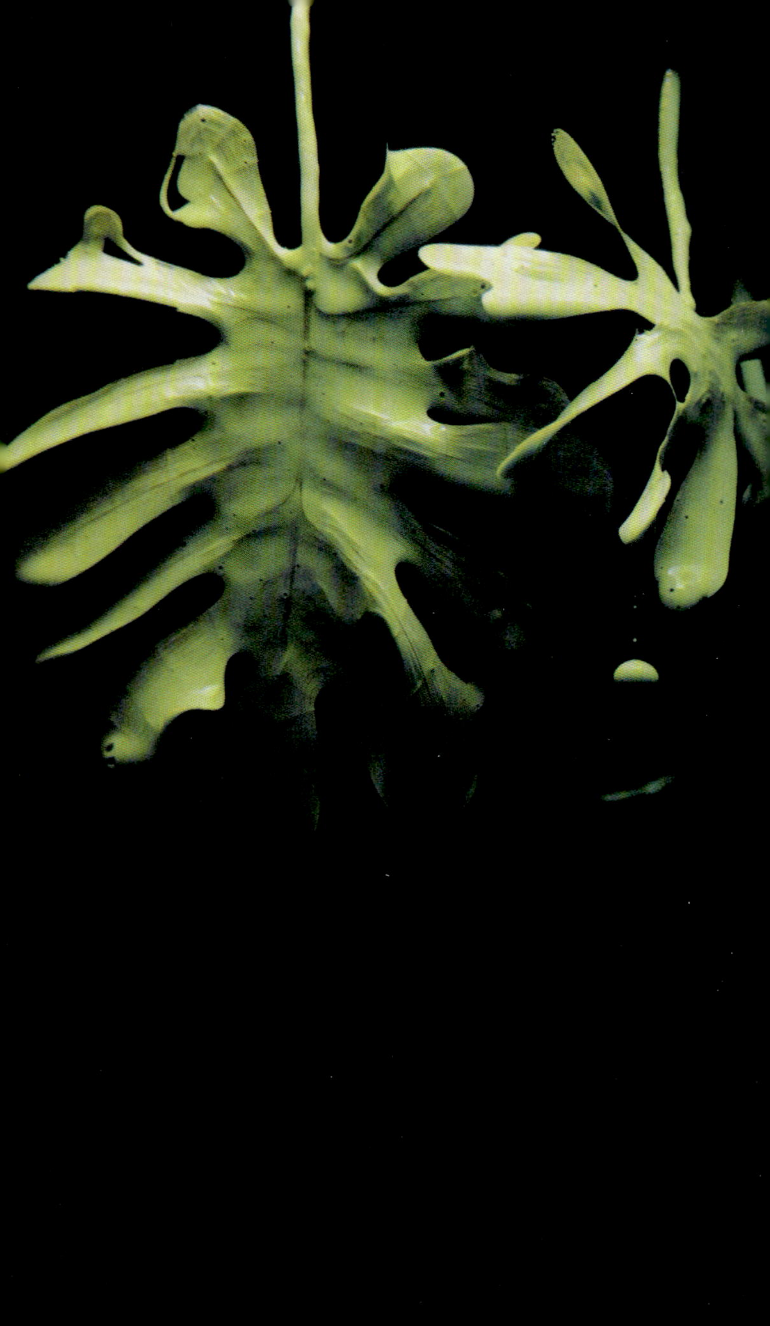

Trailer

A lie is not just in the telling. It is just as much what is un-said, such as family secrets shielded from children – that is, living a lie rather than telling one. *Trailer* relates the bizarre unravelling of such a family secret that was always waiting to be exposed. *Trailer*, in part, stems from a docu-mentary about Judy Lewis, Hollywood star and television personality Loretta Young's adoptive daughter who, in real-ity, was the illegitimate offspring of an affair between Young and Clark Gable. "What intrigues me about this story," Olde Wolbers says, "is the pretence. I am often attracted to situ-ations set in a time where facts were hidden, where people had to live keeping up appearances. I guess I have always been curious about people's families and the stories that come with them. Especially what is hidden within a family: the people who are closest to you with the biggest secrets."

Trailer differs from Olde Wolbers' earlier work, which pre-sented one ongoing location, in that its initial dissimulating set-up is divided between two scenes – the cinema and the jungle – which are not so much opposed as contrasted in their effects. Before we get to the jungle, however, there is much in common between the regimes of cinema and the hospital as the latter functions in Olde Wolbers' works. Indeed, we notice a crossover of themes between *Interloper* and *Trailer*. In his youth, *Interloper*'s narrator was subject to a bizarre experiment in isolation and sensory deprivation; the hospital became his parent and he ignored his own. In order to search for his biological parents, *Trailer*'s narrator regresses to childhood in a cinema where he "anxiously tightened his grip on the cinema seat, clutching its velvet like a monkey to its terry-cloth mother in a Harlow experiment." Cinema's cocooning effect recurs in the jungle and *Trailer*'s narrator eventually remembers being carried on his mother's hip in its lush environment. His name, Alfgar Dalio, is the same as an extinct moth, which made its cocoon-like abode in the toxic leaves of a flytrap. As such, these various images of cocooning collapse together into a metaphor for maternal protection but also for the corrosive power of the lie that remains hidden.

Trailer's narrator had walked into cinema's trap. It was just as if he followed in the footsteps of his mother, who "leaving the artificial world of cinema behind ... stepped into the deceitful theatre of plants." But first, let us step into the cinema where the strangely named Alfgar Dalio discovers his fate.

Miss Elmore Vella made her stage name immortal with her fondness …
for the flytrap's sedative gasses …
that came off its leaves as they wrapped around her tongue.
In the days of the plant's venomous reign its only enemy came in the form of a moth …
that made full use of its architecture.
Rather than being digested by the toxic leaves it would hollow them out …
transforming the plant into a cocoon that was conveniently positioned on a stalk.
With the flytrap's disappearance from the jungle the moth became homeless.
Its name, just like yours, was Alfgar Dalio.

This puzzling information came to me in the form of a trailer …
playing in a cinema in Wadena, Ohio.
A small town I had just moved to, to start a new job.
I walked out disorientated and rang my father from the phone in the lobby.
"All your mother and I were told," he answered nervously …
"was that you were a child from the hidden fallout of Hollywood.
The consequence of an on-screen glance converted to off-screen electricity …
which culminated in a paper-mâché four-poster bed …
And that you had been named Alfgar Dalio.
When you came to us we chose not to tell you that you were adopted …
as we were sure it was before the formation of your first memory."
I left the cinema in a daze.
Here is a building, I thought with curious contempt …
that is rudely broadcasting the secret of my existence every night.
Something that, up till now, had been unknown to me.
The Kinorama playhouse was the only cinema in the country …
that was still playing the Roxboro classics.
Its always-deserted interior looked like it had been dipped in the lipstick …
of the elderly lady knitting in the ticket booth.
The octogenarian proprietor circled around the cinema's exterior …
as if he were the dial on a clock.
I bravely returned the next evening …
but when the feature started I anxiously tightened my grip on the cinema seat …
clutching its velvet like a monkey to its terry-cloth mother in a Harlow experiment.
Over the course of a few years I saw all the Roxboro films.

Elmore Vella and Ring Kittle turned out to have very minor roles in these production
Their names only sometimes appeared on the credits.
Scrutinizing their mask-like over-lit faces …
I was trying to find something that was familiar or even recognizable.
But as the grain of the films became finer, bringing them closer to me …
plastic surgery pushed them further away.
Until one day I realized I had overtaken them in years …
leaving them behind their celluloid curtain in an un-aging past.
Watching the films, however, I realized a memory had slowly started to form …
And with it came an emotion forgotten since childhood.
A woman in the shape of Elmore carrying me around on her hip …
in a moist green environment.
Collecting Hummingbird eggs the size of tic-tac sweets.
Was I building fiction in the void of reality or was this an actual memory?
I decided to ask the cashier if she could tell me anything about Vella and Kittle.
Without putting down her knitting she started hesitantly:
"You won't find them on screen in colour, dear …
They disappeared in the jungle in 1922 …
where they were to star in their first feature together.
A film celebrating the invention of Kinemacolor, the old green and red stock …"
Elmore Vella was suffering from what in the profession was called the "falling eye".
In her presence sets would fold in, cameramen tripped on wires …
and whole rows of can-can dancers would keel off the stage like domino pieces.
You could say that with her condition …
it was an oversight that the studio flew her out to the Peruvian jungle.
Because after waking from her afternoon nap …
she stared out of the window of the small plane …
until she noticed the earth approaching faster and faster …
As the trees tore open its fuselage …
her seat spiralled down like a sycamore seed …
and amazingly she touched the floor almost unharmed.
She undid her seat buckle, straightened her taffeta dress …
and stepped out as if proceeding over a red carpet.
The debris of the plane was suspended in the blanket of thick vegetation above.
Magenta evening dresses and swaying tuxedos …

hung in the canopy like a cloud of butterflies.
A ghost banquet she wasn't invited to but its irrelevance was clearer than ever …
Leaving the artificial world of cinema behind …
she stepped into the deceitful theatre of plants …
Without knowing the laws of the jungle she could sense her obvious loss in its game.
For days she walked through the dark curtain of trees …
Her brain withdrawn to a trance-like now.
Her saviour came in the shape of a large tree trunk …
along which a meandering line of ants …
was still following the contours of a long gone obstruction.
Unaware that a change had taken place which forced them down this peculiar route initially,
they had created a temporary moving negative …
It was that of a man slumped against a tree with a large sombrero.
She knew it was the contour of her co-lead, Ring Kittle;
a handsome man who had barely made it from silent to spoken …
as he suffered badly from verbal vertigo.
She followed the line of ants until it halted at his trailer.
He had obviously found the wreckage of the plane already …
As he was reeling strips of celluloid into a noxious bonfire.
"The camphor keeps the mosquitoes away," …
she heard him say as she passed out in his arms.
He carried her to the four-poster bed he had assembled from the debris.
They waited for months for news from the studio …
But as the jungle fenced them in just as the much longed for stardom would have …
the fickle gods of filmdom had other plans …
Finally a local man from a nearby river settlement came …
to announce that Technicolor had been invented.
So funds got shifted and the project cancelled.
As the man entered their trailer …
his taxonomic eye fell immediately on the flytrap plants strewn across the floor.
"Coxocotl …" he exclaimed, a species long lost to his generation.
A plant with mildly hallucinogenic qualities …
that his elders had taken in their continuous search for visual peace …
in the densely leafed jungle.
Elmore explained that she had been picking them from the crash site …

where young saplings had sprung up out of the giant ashtray.
The plane had upturned the earth and given seeds …
that lay dormant there for 50 years the chance to bud.
Her Hollywood nose for opiates had her crash the plane …
on the jungle's oldest natural barbiturates.
The man's tribe decided to rename the plant in her honour …
Not aware that her habit would single-handedly make it extinct again …
and leave the Alfgar Dalio moth whose life depended on it homeless.

I didn't need to ask the lady how she knew all this.
How she could have witnessed the un-witnessable.
I figured that both she and Mister Kittle must have known back then …
that their reappearance could never compete …
with their almost mythical disappearance …
Vanishing had been a good career move.
But leaving what was only ever a very dim limelight behind …
had obviously become their greatest torment.
Not the jungle and its unpredictable character …
but the meaninglessness of not being observed.

This conclusion – the meaninglessness of not being observed
– must be thought in all its senses, from the "point of view"
of the cinema and the jungle and all their "protagonists."
Cinema and jungle are secret sharers, not isolated moments
of the narrative passage. Moreover, the relationship of the
terms to each other (of "meaninglessness" to "observation")
potentially is varied. One has an intentional structure
(observation being therefore meaningful) and the other
not (meaningless but having an effect, nonetheless, as a
signal rather than a sign). For instance, in the jungle, where
camouflage is a device of deceit or protection, not being
observed is a strategy for survival, whereas in Hollywood
it is a death sentence. Within the jungle, however, there is

just as much competition for visibility – think of mating and reproduction. There is no opposition here of cinema and jungle that would stand for visibility and invisibility respectively. This would only be the point of view – or problem, lost or forgotten in the jungle – of Elmore Vella and Ring Kittle and their Hollywood regime. Throughout the narrative, we find a crossover between cinema's regime and the jungle's realm where natural and artificial are inverted in their values. Nature is a "deceitful theatre of plants." And it is in the cinema, after all, that Alfgar Dalio learns his jungle story.

Visibility is not the subject here. A lure, visibility only misleads us. *Trailer* is a narrative for us as much as it is for Alfgar Dalio. In it he learns not only his history but also the origin of his name. This, then, is Alfgar's narrative: both his story and the story he tells. From the beginning, it is a story of observation and nomination in which the world of plants seemingly is more meaningful than Hollywood constellations. The narrative starts where plants "compete with one another outside of their awareness" in the Amazonian jungle in which "three species stood out self-consciously." These species are not real, of course, but exist only within this story. They are Ring Kittle, Elmore Vella, and Alfgar Dalio, the names of species as well as, we find out eventually, of members of a human family. Observed and classified, these species of plants and moth have an identity and a place within a system of knowledge and reference. They stand out, have an identity and a place, something the human Alfgar does not, it seems, possess as he soon finds out (contrary to Judy Lewis's discovery) that he is adopted. All security of family dissipates and he finds himself as if homeless like the poor Alfgar Dalio moth.

He rudely learns this secret, which potentially is known to all, through a film trailer obscurely playing in an American Midwest movie theatre. Its strobing projection mimicks that of a rescue signal beamed from the dense, all-absorbing jungle, but it is destined solely for him. The narrative proceeds from an alternation of film presentation and enquiry, what he is given to see and then asks about. From the accident of this cinematic encounter, Alfgar immediately questions his father, then deliberately seeks out and scrutinizes the old Roxboro classics for clues to his origins, which play in this same fossilized theatre from the gilded era of Hollywood movie palaces. His search through these outdated films inverts the trailer's search for him. In the celluloid blur of the deserted cinema, he is stirred, perhaps, by a memory of his jungle childhood and asks himself, "Was I building fiction in the void of reality or was this an actual memory?" Finally, he questions the cinema's ticket seller. Witness to the unwitnessable, the ticket seller tells him a fantastic tale.

Was his emotion a memory or an effect of cinema? No longer vanished obscurities, the cinema's proprietors now operate a cinematic apparatus: whether as an archive of their insignificance or of the technological demise of a medium, or as a lure to capture this young man, we do not know. We only have these images and the narrative to guide us where we, too, become witness to the unwitnessable. It is impossible to know the status of the images we see. The red and green sequences are not so much referential to the actualities of cinema interior and jungle vegetation that they depict and that alternate in the screening, as they are the technological separation

of the red and green film stock of the Kinemacolor process
– the short-lived, two-colour film process that is the only
historical fact in this fiction. (Then again, what Hollywood
hallucination are *we* contributing by projecting past studio
portrayals of the jungle?) Are the differing jungle sequences
repeated screenings of the trailer or are they the slow
evocation of Alfgar's memories? At this point a subtle
narrative shift occurs where we are not certain whether
Alfgar reports the ticket-taker's speech or fills in the story
from his memory. After all, Alfgar is the narrator: we learn
every strange turn of this fantastic, Borgesian story from
his voice-over. Perhaps he assumes this narrative in order
to claim his identity. His identity may be nothing other than
this story he seeks out *or* makes up, this fiction unrolling
before us. Perhaps he fabricates even the trailer in his
mind as a fantasy that his real parents are looking for him
and have not, as he now has discovered, abandoned him.

In this scenario as author of the narrative, Alfgar begins
his story with what is most important to him, the unity of a
family circle: his fantasy origin in an Edenic setting where
he also receives his name. In the taxonomic splendour of
the jungle, he is reunited with his original family, *the* original family who are at the origin of nomination (their own
names are given to species: that is, to the three species
standing out self-consciously). But as he only imagines
this – or needs to imagine this – through the shock of his
discovery that he is adopted, he must account for both this
discovery and his abandonment.

The discovery is complicated by also being a deceit. A
positive light, moreover, must be cast upon both the dis-

covery *and* the abandonment. The story Alfgar then continues to make up, therefore, is conflicted between desire and revenge: his desire to find his original parents and his desire now for revenge against them. He makes up the story that the ticket-taker, whom he now turns into his birth mother, reputedly tells. (His story repeats the quest structure of the fairy tale, where the protagonist finds that he is a prince hidden by his royal parents in woods or left with peasants for his protection. But Alfgar's story is also told through the fabrications of film characters, plots, images, and settings of (a degraded) Hollywood film history, much like the camp or pastiche productions of 1960s American underground film of Andy Warhol, Jack Smith, etc.). Alfgar must fabricate the notion that his parents are looking for him – that they lost him through some accident – at the same time that he makes of these incidents the ruin of their career. The narrative arc starts out in the trailer with self-conscious standing-out and ends in the ensuing narrative as the meaninglessness of not being observed. The former was the result of the family being together; the latter was a result of their separation, with his parents' obscurity the cost of their abandonment of their son. The abandoned and flooded cinema portrayed at the conclusion is also a revenge on cinema, one other consequence of Alfgar's love-hate relationship to his parents.[2]

The term through which this transition from visibility to obscurity is negotiated in this narrative is deceit, but not as the story's subject or content. Itself obscured and obscuring, deceit accounts for the conflict, or contradictions, in the construction of the story, that is, Alfgar's construction of *his* story. The conflict within the story is played out as a conflict between the two elements of the work that we hear and see, between its word and image tracks. Narrative and cinema are opposed, not by the artist Saskia Olde Wolbers but by the "author," Alfgar Dalio. Narrative is the art of origins (his desired origins) while cinema, from which Alfgar constructs the story, is an art of deceit. Not just subject to this Hollywood history and subject to film, in revenge Alfgar has made his own film, an underground film. Like Olde Wolbers, he has constructed his own fiction and his own film from the elements of image and voice-over. A stand-in for the artist, perhaps, he must be the fabricator of a whole, not a participant within a part.

Deadline

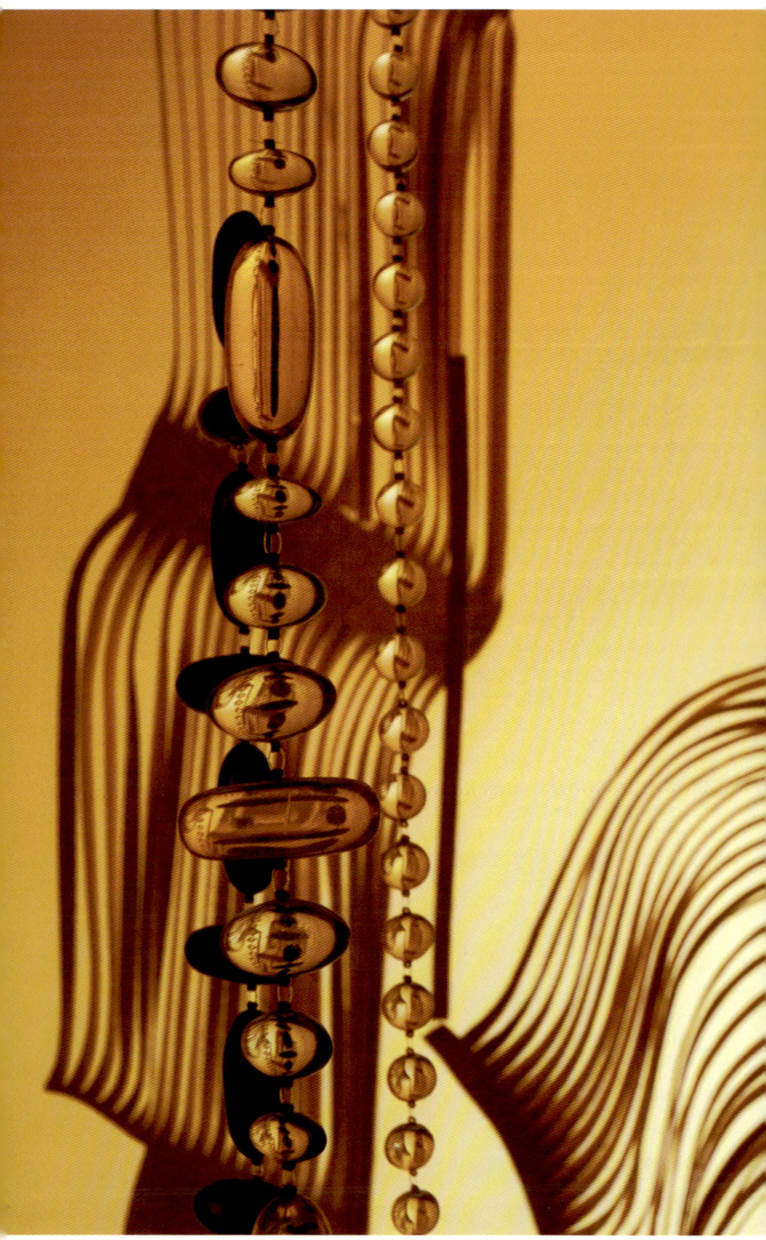

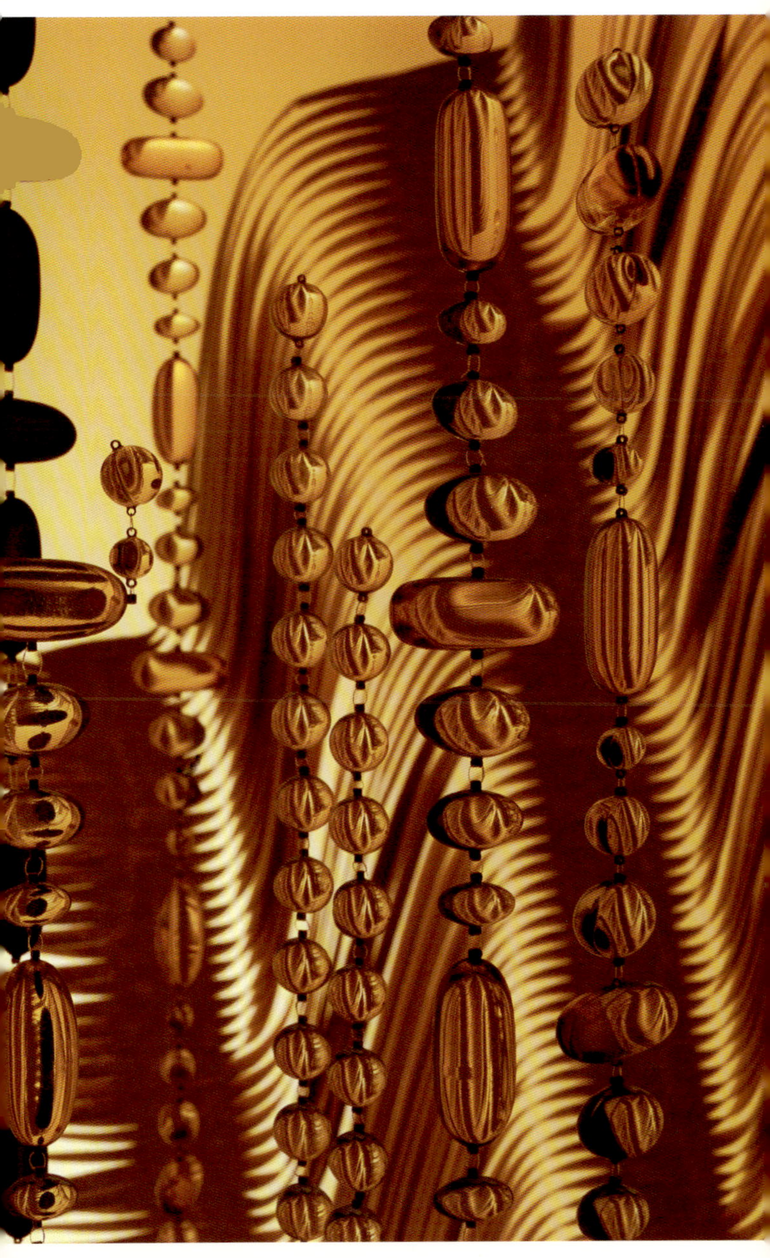

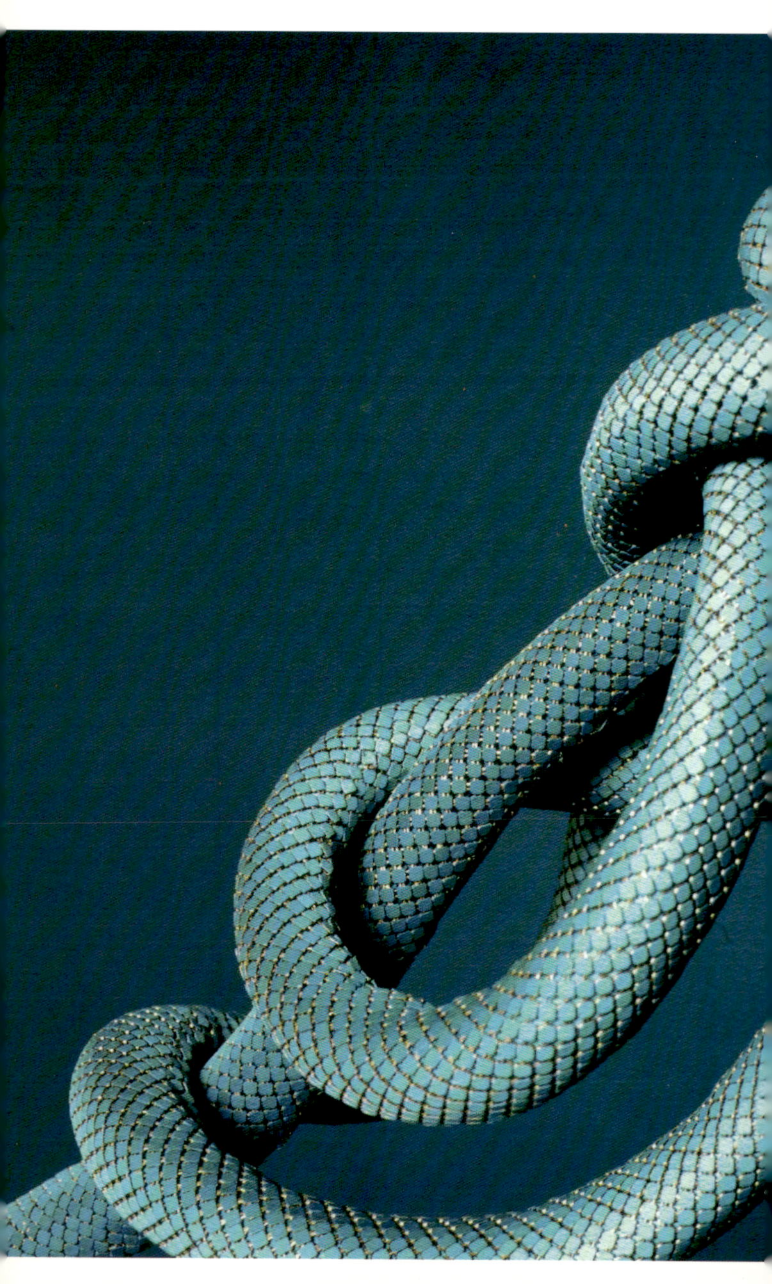

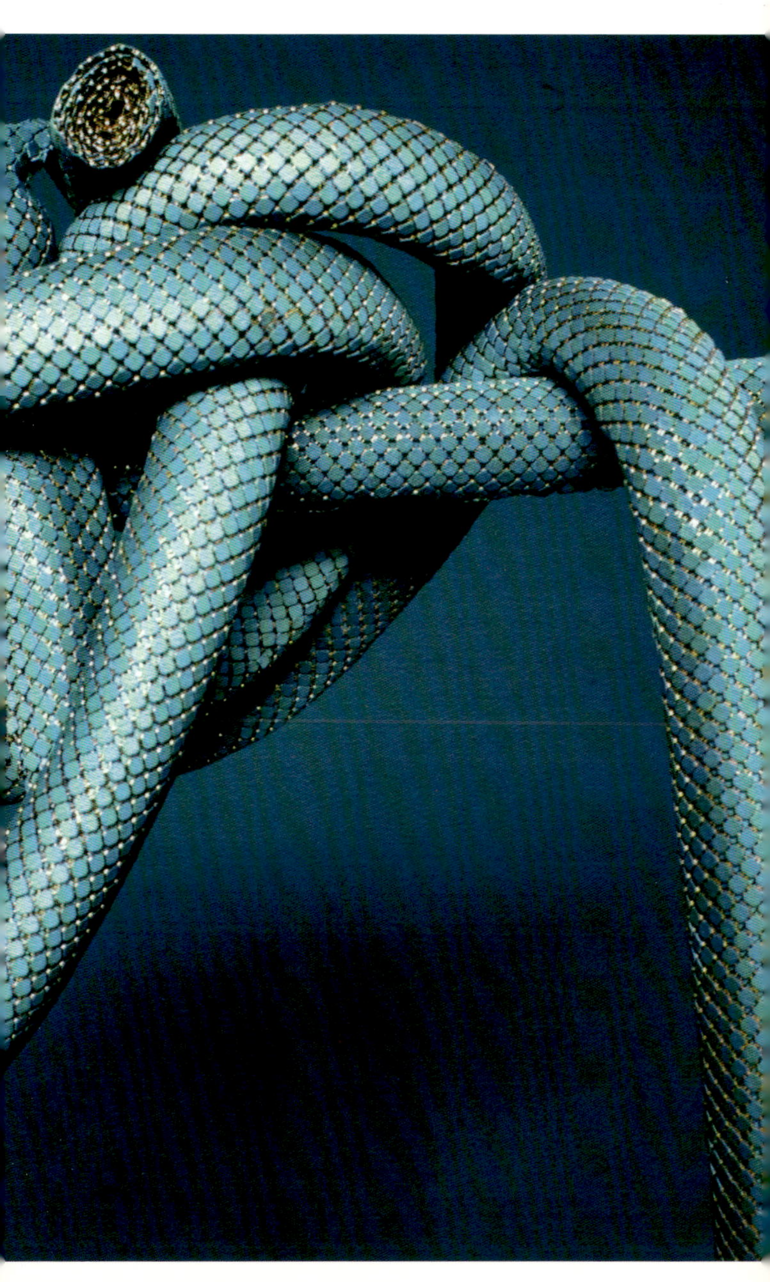

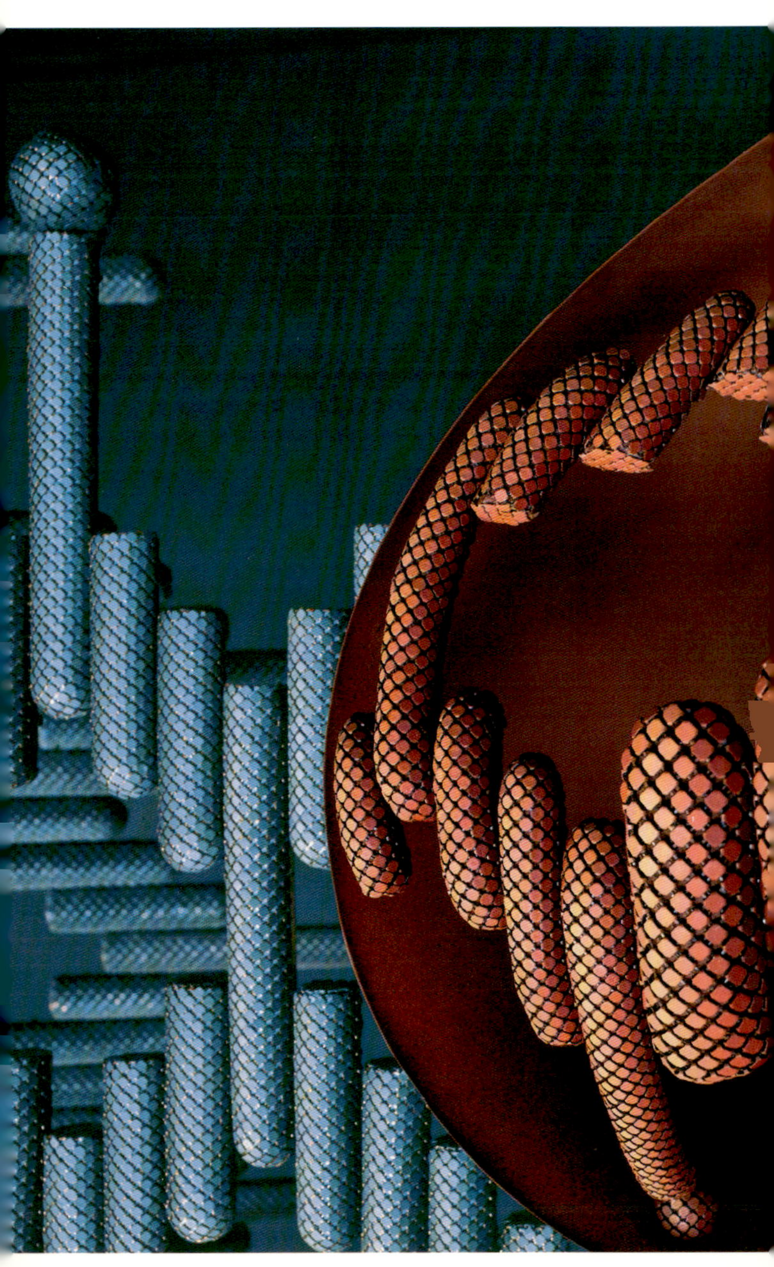

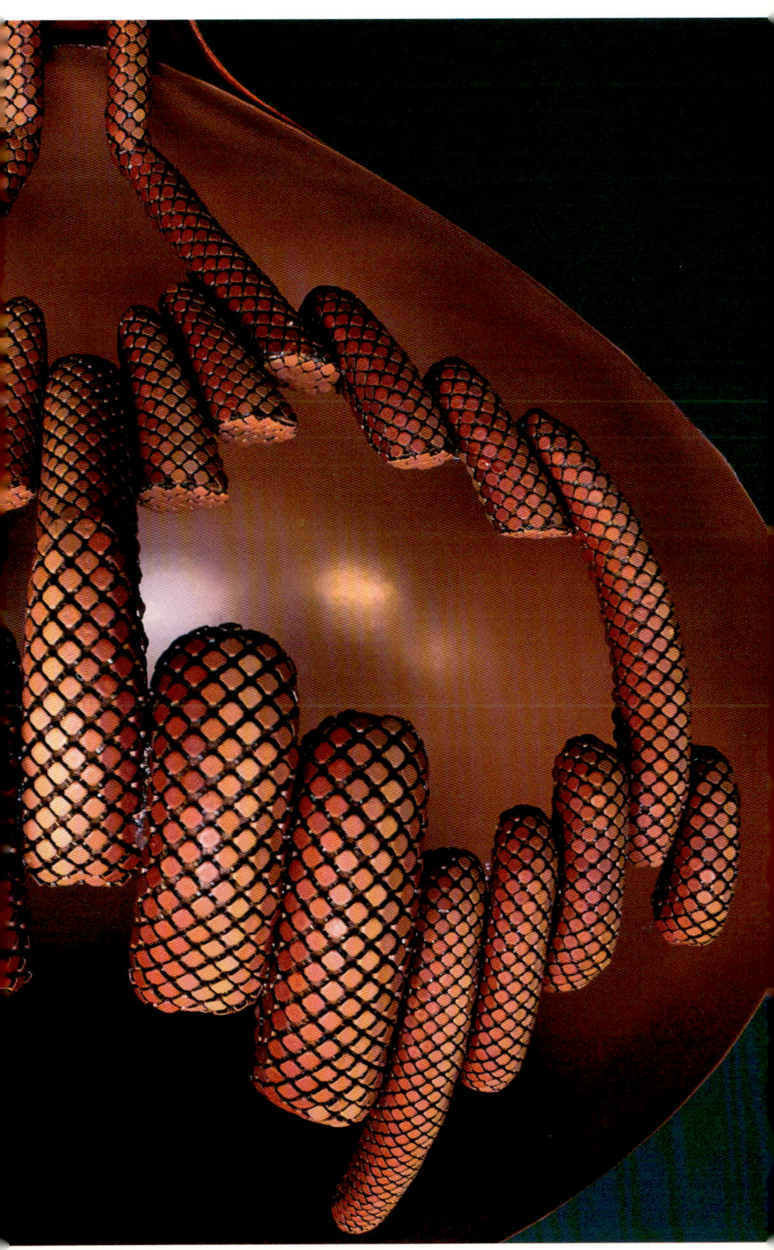

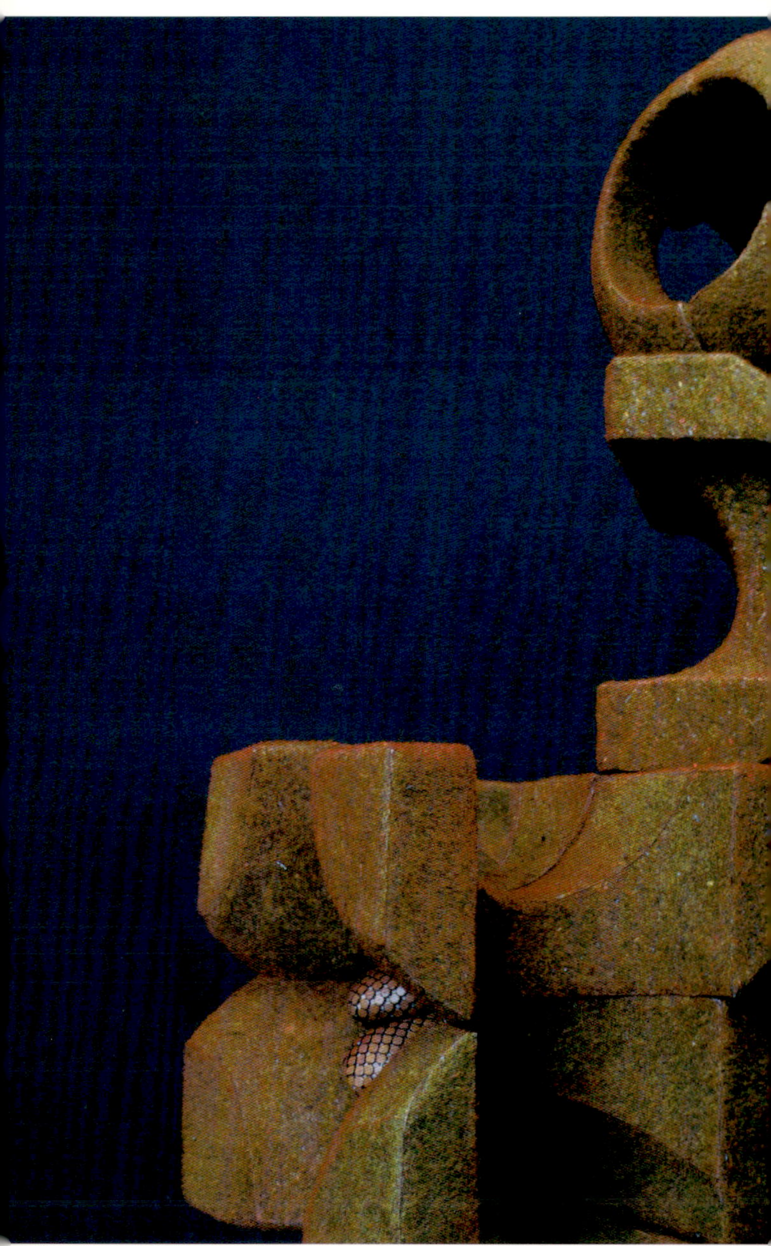

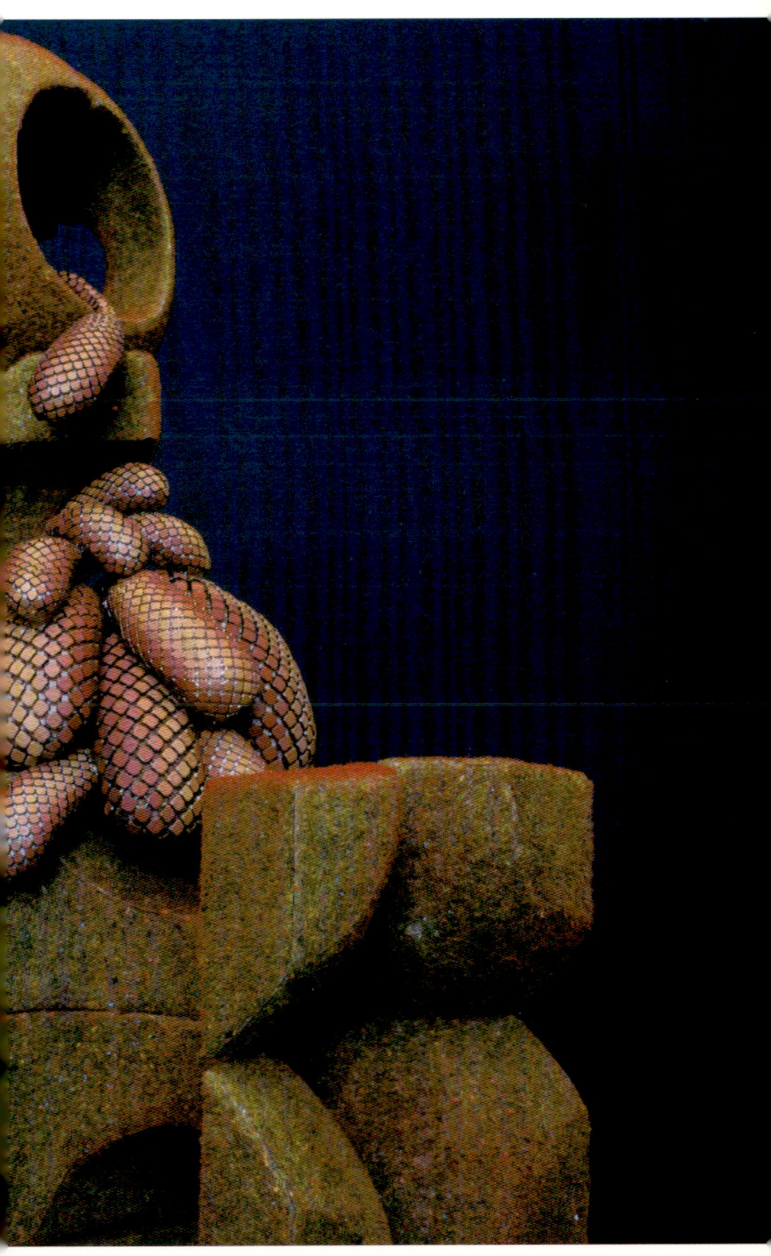

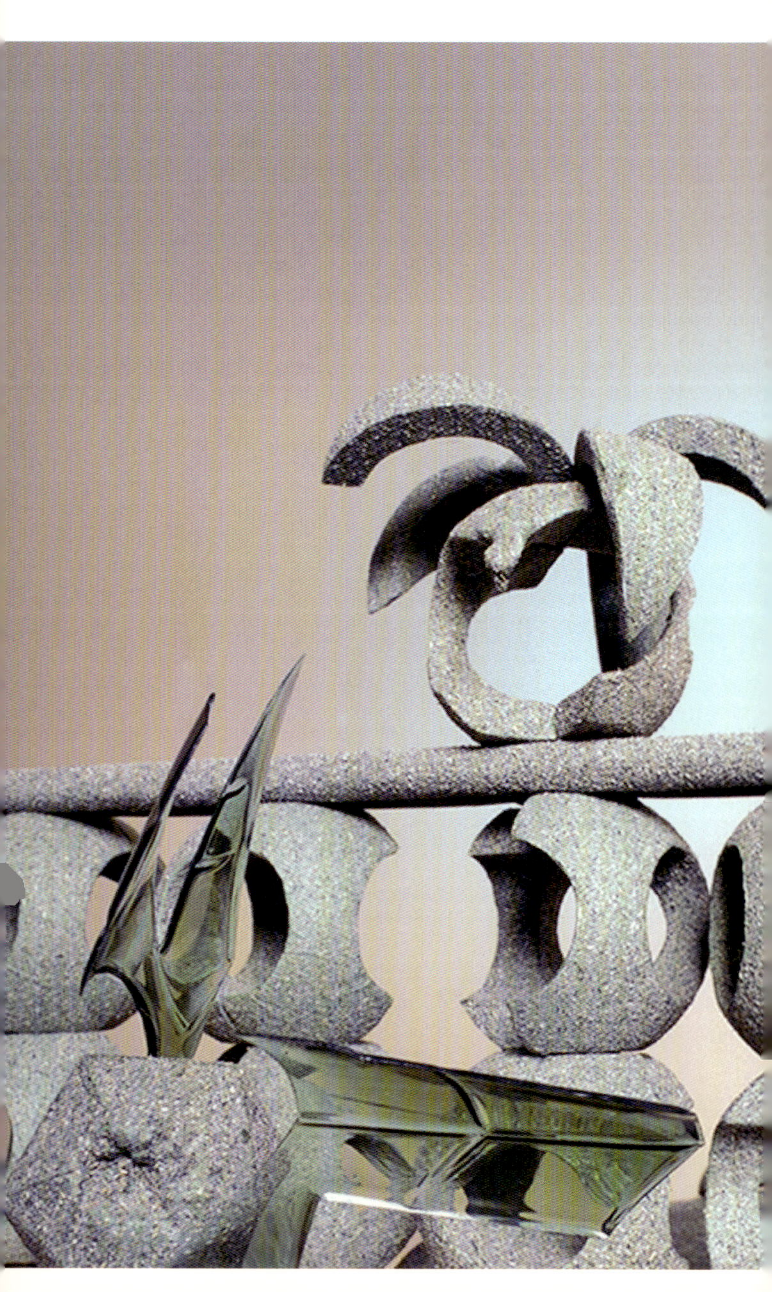

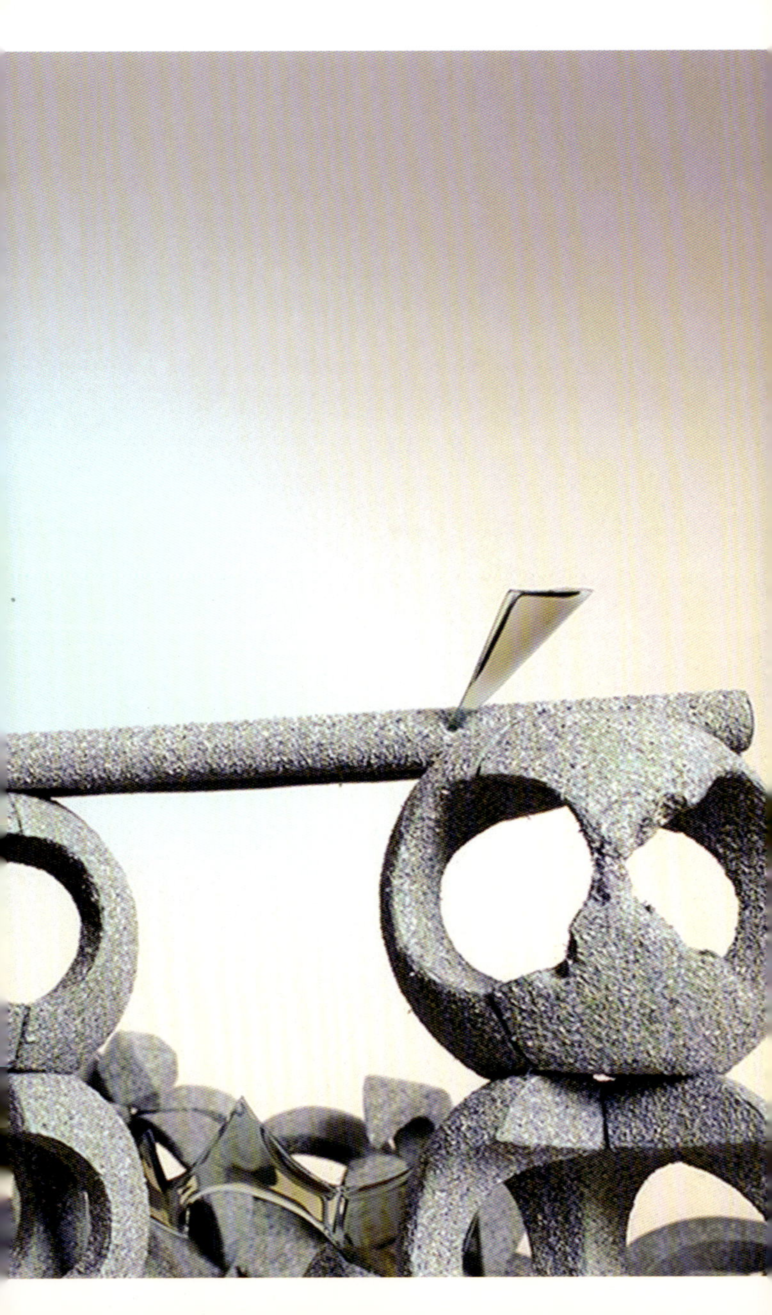

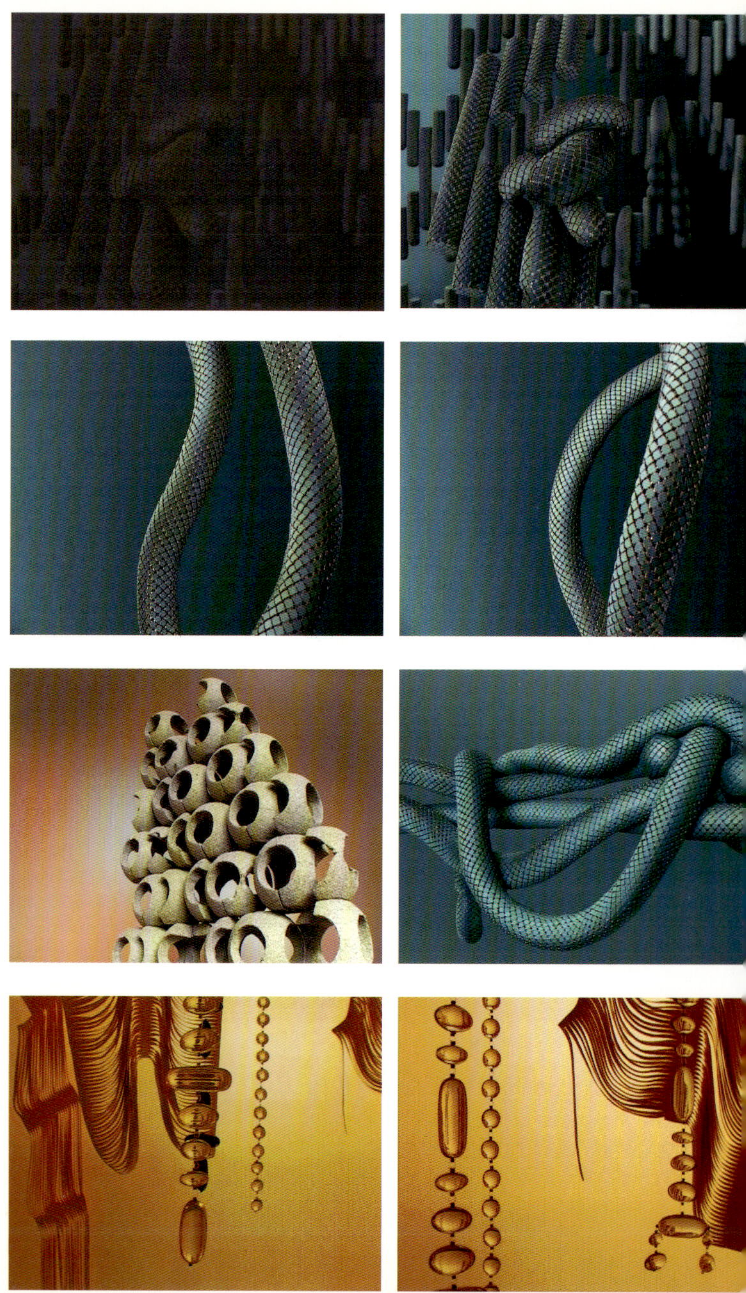

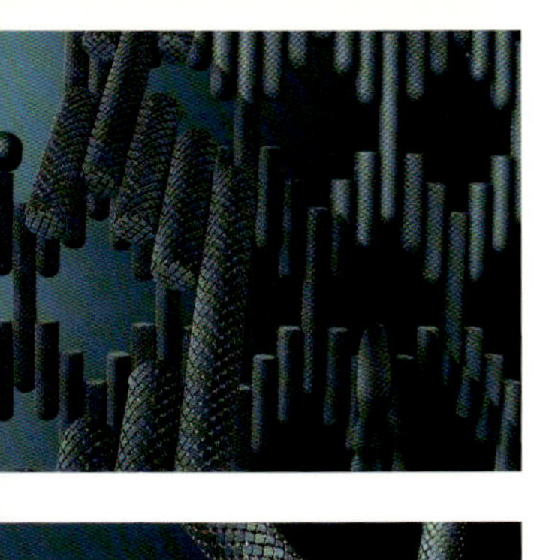
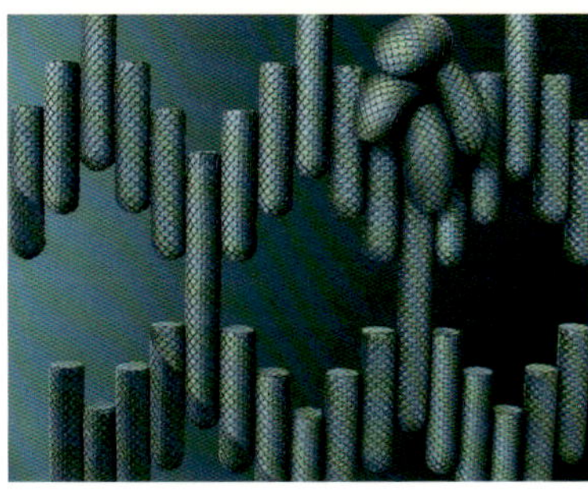
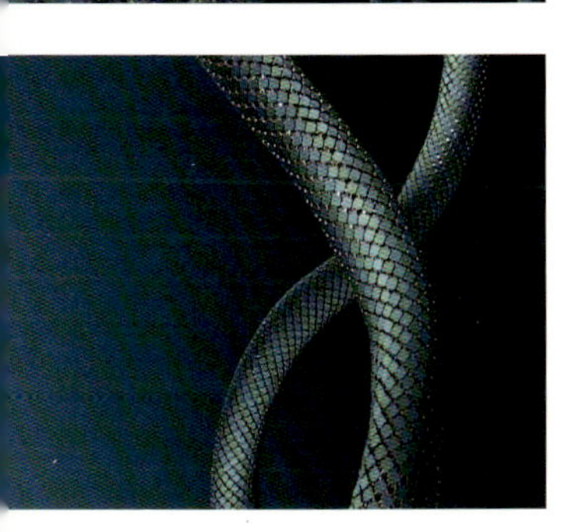
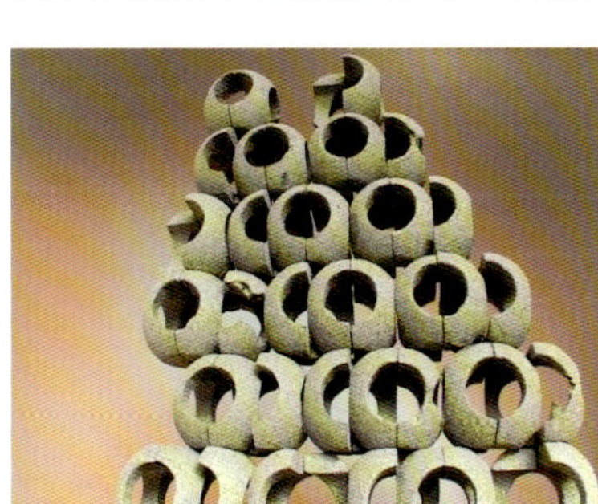
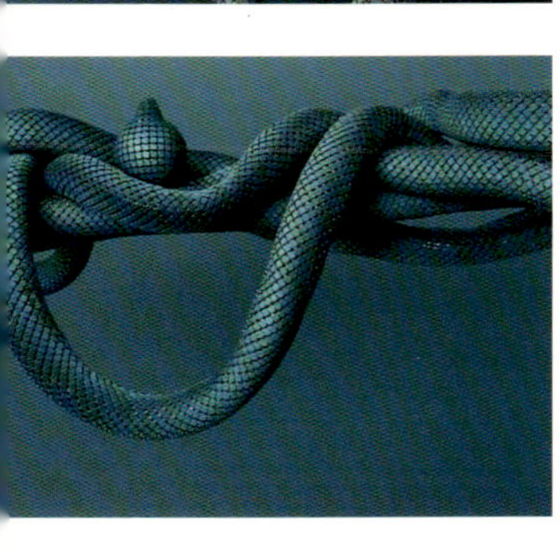
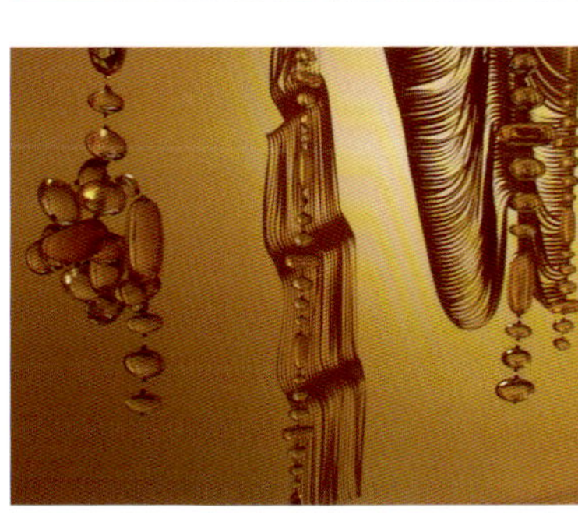
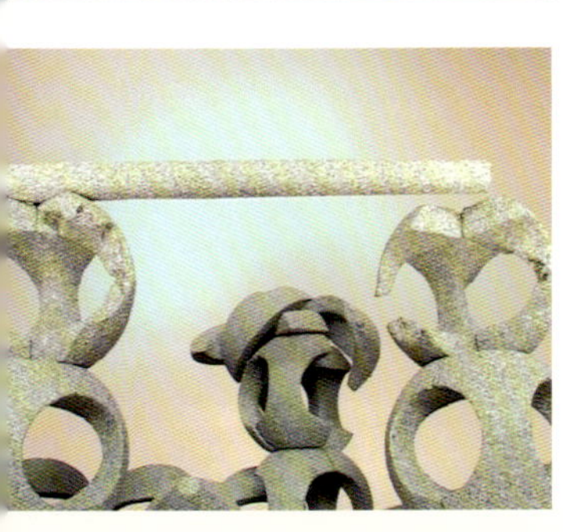
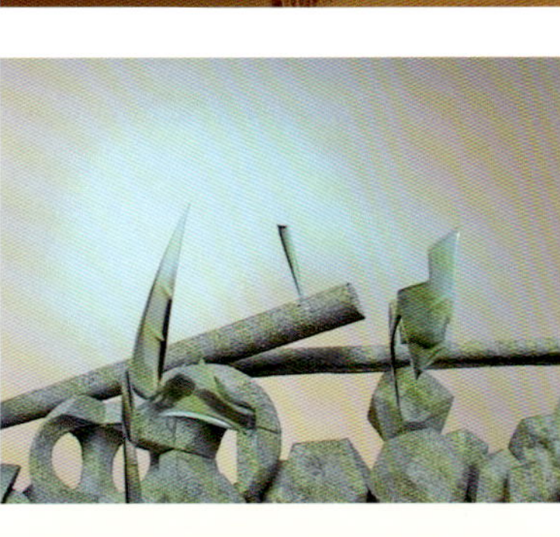

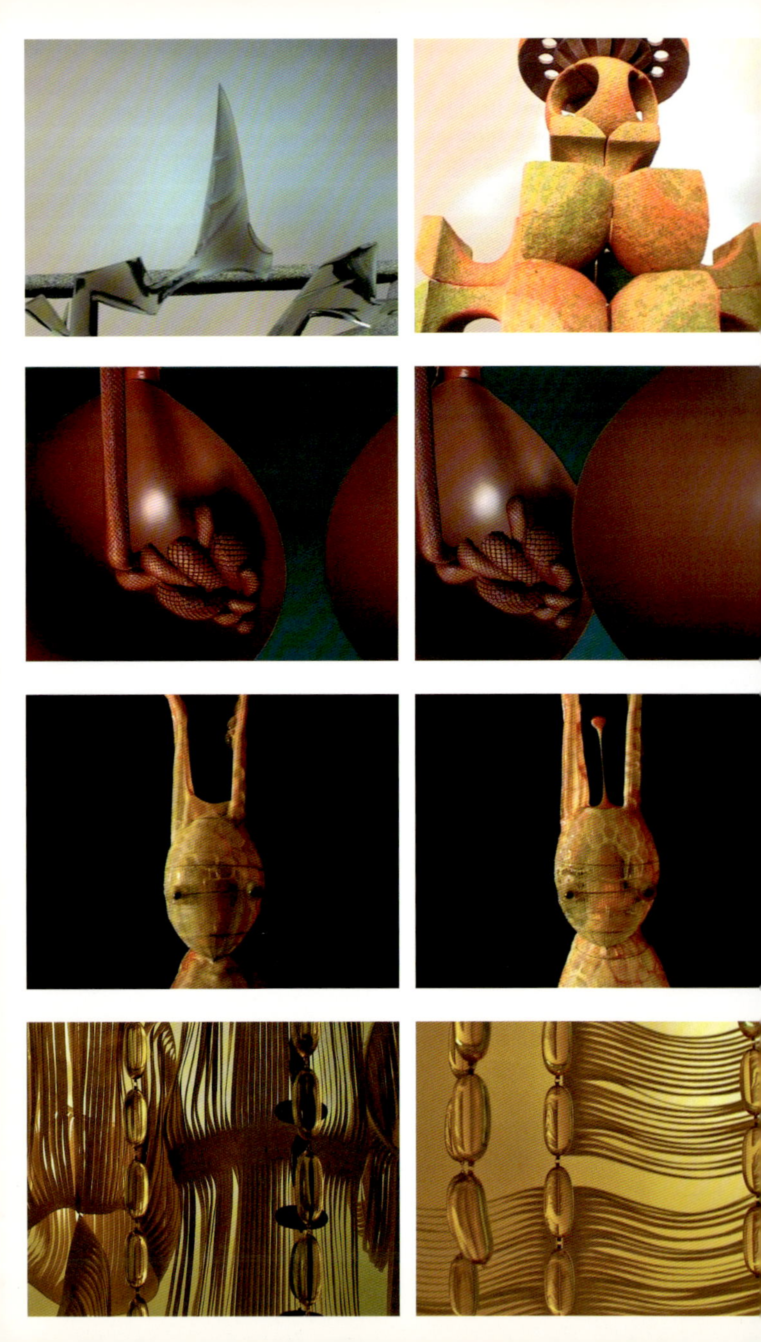

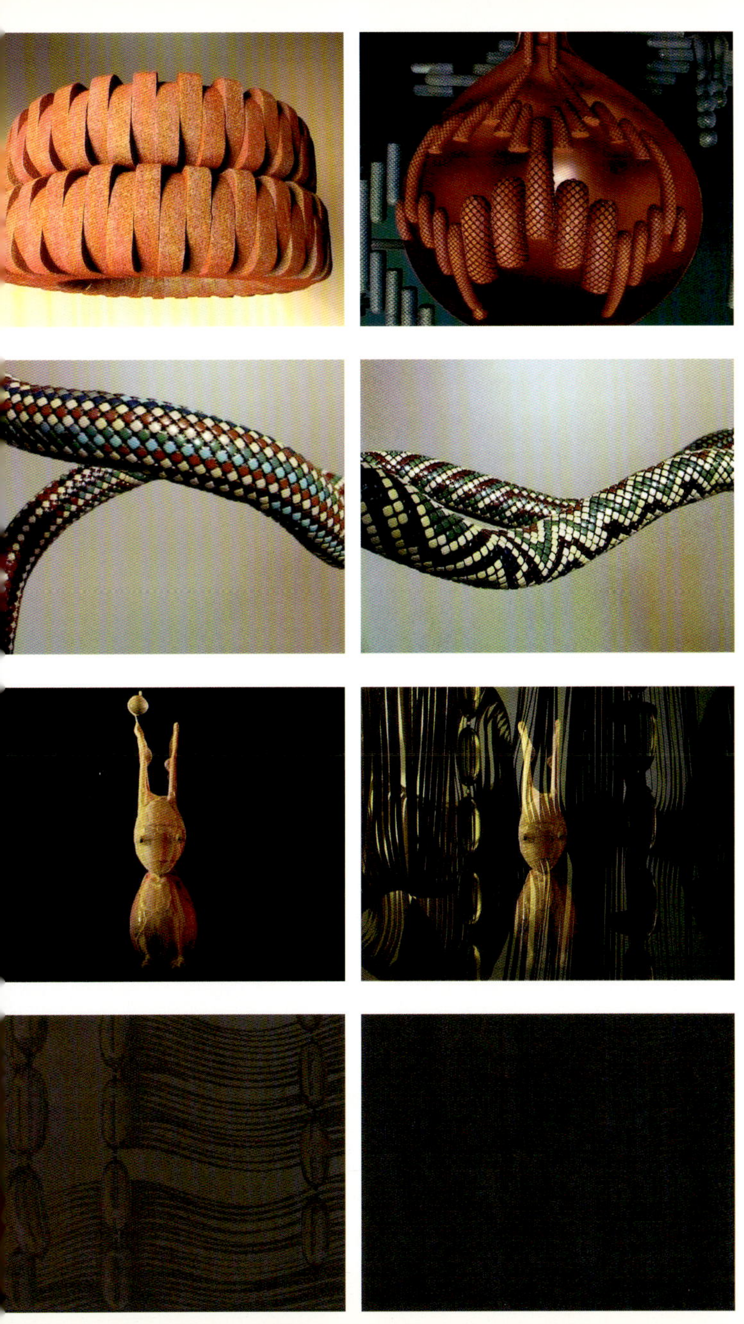

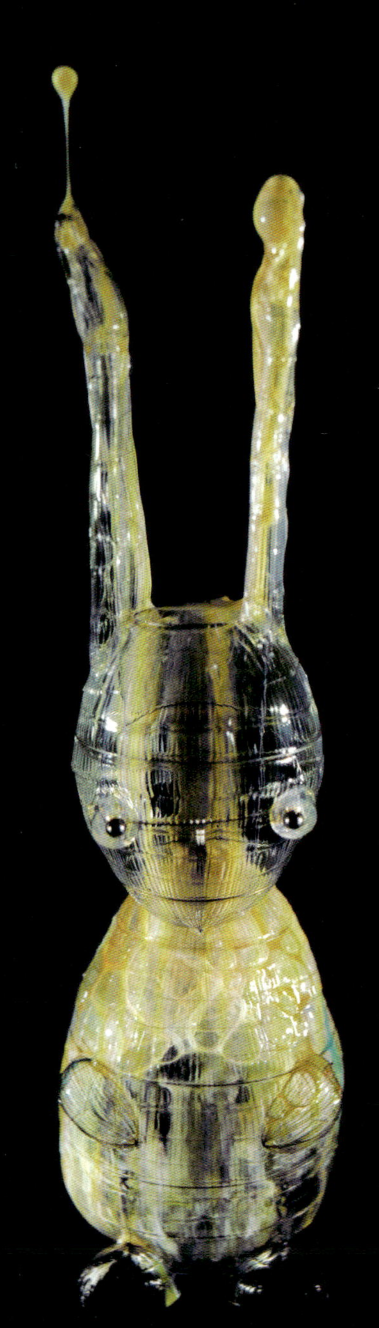

Deadline

Towards the end of *Deadline*, in an airport terminal after a
long journey, the narrator is greeted by "a smiling stranger
who yet looks so familiar" and who holds under his arm a
book whose cover renders all the elements of this young
woman's preceding voyage as if its predestination: "Do I see
rightly under his arm a book, with on the cover a photograph
of father's bush-taxi? And the title *Deadline*, by Lamin the
first Bojang. Underneath in smaller italic letters a quote I
think, 'Do we all have journeys mapped out in our central
nervous systems like migrating birds? It seems the only way
to account for our insane restlessness.' And in even smaller
letters, 'The remarkable story of an epic voyage undertaken
by a man in his desire to travel away from the everyday
squalor of his region, that sees him drive a bush taxi from his
native Gambia to an airport in Nigeria in a failed attempt to
catch a plane to Greece. He spends sixteen months on the
road working his way through eight West African countries.'"

The narrative returns on itself, unless it starts here, for this, basi-
cally, is a précis of the story we just heard. Here it is in full:

I found myself very far away from home …
Father had driven us slowly east … in a rattling van …
After we traveled almost 3000 miles … we parted …
And I boarded a plane to fly 8 hours north … over matt black deserts …

Whose tiny settlements looked imprisoned by their fierce surroundings.
At my destination, I was welcomed by the exact same man …
who had earlier waved me off.
These were of course not totally the same man …
But my father and my uncle had very similar features.
What told them apart were their surroundings and attire.
While father wore his hair in short dreads, a crisp England shirt …
suit jacket and Sta-Prest slacks …
My uncle came to the airport in Athens fully wrapped in traditional robes …
Finely starched into a neat angular sketch of a human form.
Forty-three years ago my grandfather's two wives …
had each delivered him a son.
On the very same day … in the exact same hour …
lying in adjacent rooms of their compound.
Father and uncle were twins with the luxury …
of having grown in their mothers alone.
Although the exact timing was fiercely disputed …
Both women stubbornly called their sons Lamin … the first-born.
But as my uncle was thought to be 3 weeks overdue …
and my father a week early … Uncle was appointed the elder …
and Father had his fate randomly sealed by a mere guess.
The year was 1960 …
and the Japanese had just built a large cold store on our beach.
An indigo pagoda holding shark-fins …
Men conquered their immense fear of the violent sea.
But while some had returned from the capital with a business degree …
Drifting through the deep sea for weeks on end …
beating hammerhead sharks with sticks … were the only jobs going.
We became a destination … for tourists to nostalgically find a way of life …
that had long left their own surroundings.
The army was formed and uncle, being the eldest …
was sent to the military academy at Yundum,
while father reluctantly stayed fishing.
My uncle was sent to Liberia as part of the African peace keeping forces …
The growing tourist industry acted as a natural Stellenbosch …

for most soldiers upon their return.
Uncle became head of security … at the large hotel complex
a Libyan had erected in the next bay.
Here Soldiers patrolled the beach …
keeping a very mild eye on hawkers … blind beggars and children …
often their own … Selling bits of airplane meals …
or complimentary soaps from neighbouring hotels.
Crime was virtually unheard of in this region …
But the tourists almost expected it …
And only felt at home if they were protected.
The hotel, however … was plagued by an absence of locals …
As the owner had foolishly built his venture upon the terrain …
Of the much revered bush-dragon.
I should not really be talking of this creature …
But Ninki Nanka is something snakelike on a horse …
With the head of a termite carrying a small diamond on its cranium.
It is born from one egg in the middle of a clutch of python eggs,
But apart from the professional dragon slayers no one knows this for sure …
As your skin will peel off as soon as its gaze rests upon you.
Tourists waved the tales of the fatalistic beast away …
But even they sensed a presence in the hotel gardens.
The management eagerly concealed the fact …
that the hotel really had no constant electricity.
And where electricity is not …
fear instead jitters through the humid edible nights.
I remember spending an evening there as a child.
Uncle's room was painted a bright yellow …
He proudly gave me a guided tour of his life by shining a torch
over a row of photos on the wall.
Various women in stylish boubous, slanting off velvety aubergine shoulders …
smiled at us:
His ex-wife, his ex-girlfriend, another ex-girlfriend … and his new fiancé …
who had disappeared.
They were arranged in fading order of engagement.
Photographed against the yellow backdrop upon which they now hung.

Posing on the same tan leather sofa from where I sat watching them.
The last in the series was a photo of the sofa itself.
But no new lady was to fill this image as the hotel closed down soon after.
And my uncle moved to Greece with one of the European woman …
Who had been returning annually for some African company …
Father was obliged to marry his brother's abandoned fiancé.
Love is a luxury that didn't apply to either situation …
Soon after giving birth to my brother our mother died.
And father retreated to a house … at the far end of our town's palm fringed bay.
Here his solitude seemed amplified by the fact that his house …
Was the sole broadcaster of an electric light into the Gunjur beach night sky.
Daily we spotted him going into the sea by sand dune mosque …
And watched him shrink to a tiny black dot,
As he swam a dangerously long way straight into the turbulent grey mass.
My brother and I lived at mama Manlafi's compound …
We called her grandmother … but there were at least 6 generations between us.
She was born around 1860 a time when cannonballs …
Were lazily shot from a gunship as it travelled up-river mapping out territory.
Gravity defined The Gambia's new borders …
And they echo every bend and curve in the river … 20 km to the north and south.
Grandmother was an archive of stories immaculately remembered.
Constantly retold to keep snakes at bay …
She talked of a time before there were roads … of slave capturing …
and miracle cures.
We know details of her wedding night …
Her first trip to the sea … early strangers in their cage-like hotels …
And the subsequent war over eggs as the demand for these quite inedible
things soared.
Generations coiled into one another … like rings round a tree.
Events furthest away in her past are freshest in her memory.
The present a far away planetary system …
Our departure a fading star …
Father's bush-taxi had the word Deadline painted on its sides …
A Logo belonging to another world.
We joined the ongoing parade of vehicles …

circling round the turntable through the soft sand.
Sunken station wagons weighed down by the heat, passengers …
and their luggage.
Large fish on luggage racks, chickens in clusters on the bonnet …
and even a coffin perched on a roof.
In answer to where we were going he evasively replied …
This van has crossed the Sahara …
and will now help us further towards our goal … god willing.
He appointed us with our on board functions …
My brother, learner driver … me, the controller of tickets …
and himself, the head driver.
During the day passengers sat silently facing straight ahead …
as if in standby mode.
At night my brother drove … while we balanced on the thin metal benches
welded to the floor.
In our sleep we felt people materialize in the glare of our headlights.
Side-mirrors brushed against heavy garments and rusty machetes …
furtively clicked the sides.
When both awake we played our usual road-game …
where our index finger controlled a very long imaginary saw blade …
that extended from the side of the van.
Slicing through trees and shrubs along the road and lifting up suddenly …
But not always successfully, when we passed people.
Father did not like our game much and was concerned by my brothers commentary …
That revealed a rather blood thirsty imagination.
Among the hand painted posters on his side of our bedroom …
One showed a snake coming out of a women's vagina vomiting money …
Another, Mr. Swampthing eating coins
These examples of bloodthirsty modern-day alchemy …
were ads for the Nigerian video-nasties,
That were popular in our small cinderblock cinema on days we had electricity.
But driving through this arid foreign landscape …
our bedroom seemed very far away.
The milometer had long reached its limit and was now counting backwards.
We entered worlds in our game that we had not seen before.

109

Sawing down the odd straggly palm and gravity defying glass buildings.
Husks of recent heydays.
Illegal petrol stations sprang up in the form of large glass vessels …
Filled with a deep orange essence.
Like photo lenses they inverted the landscape …
Providing a glimpse of an upside down netherworld.
They announced the nearing of our destination …
the gargantuan oil-state ahead … Nigeria.
In Lagos father was to board a plane for Athens …
to reunite with his estranged brother.
As always a manly silence clouded the subject of his brother.
Perhaps because their past was something of a misunderstanding.
The fate of their lives could have so easily been swapped …
So often hidden behind memory is the undefined relationship with one self …
A vaguely remembered half-stranger … a parasite.
Our journey had seen us follow the road that hugged the intestinal river to
Basse-Sante …
Crossing through Cassamance into Middle and Upper Guinea.
Here the river ended …
and we navigated the blinding dry lands of Sikasso and Burkina Faso.
We followed Zemis that flew past us like bats …
Their drivers lying across saddles …
legs stretched out behind them to gain speed.
On to northern Ghana, Togo and Benin,
Where one night I was woken by a sudden change in direction …
My brother was at the wheel and our vehicle was reversing.
After 200 yards our headlights lit a small heap of fur …
We had struck a rabbit.
He got out of the cab and slit its throat …
Announcing breakfast as he threw its limp body in the back of the van.
Very soon after we were stopped again …
This time by a man, waving frantically.
His front teeth were pulled and his hair was shaved at the sides …
in a flattop style.
Simgam was a long distance heavy lorry driver …

the most dangerous vehicle on the road …
Often driven wildly by kola-nut chewing drivers.
He had now lost his truck and its contents while asleep under the cab.
His motor-mate was to keep an eye out for the night raiders …
But as he had also disappeared it was obviously him who had stolen the truck.
Although illiterate, Simgam added 5 local dialects to our repertoire …
And became our guide through a country he knew very well.
On the 7th of May 2003 we finally reached the Nigerian border.
Where armed customs officers inspected our car …
Father and Simgam were inexplicably retained …
Until at dusk a Roundlight Mercedes appeared from behind the border.
Out stepped a large rotund man in a white lace tunic …
On it a pattern so elaborate …
that I thought I could see the Eiffel tower in its folds …
This was Simgam's boss.
He greeted the guards in a familiar fashion,
Touching foreheads three ways … as Simgam was released.
Father was to be fined 10.000 naira for attempting to import a dead rabbit.
Money he did not have …
He wrapped his bottle of Na-so liquid that had balanced on the dashboard
for the entire journey.
It held the magic words of his juju-clerk …
poured from a pen onto paper in a pan.
Stirred with belief and distilled into a potent notch to keep evil at bay.
This was handed to me along with a Nigerian passport …
that of Simgam's deceased wife.
I was instructed: Salingding you go … you can travel …
you can be my eyes … we will wait.
So here I am in a vacuum-sealed air-conditioned airport.
In front of a smiling stranger that yet looks so familiar …
Do I see rightly under his arm a book …
with on the cover a photograph of father's bush-taxi?
And the title, Deadline, by Lamin the first Bojang?
Underneath in smaller italic letters a quote I think
"Do we all have journeys mapped out in our central nervous systems …

Here we are again as if in a trap – set in the receding frames of a linguistic *mis-en-abyme*. Of course, we notice that, between its opening and conclusion, the narrative naturally amplifies itself, reproducing what might be found within the covers of this book.[3] Perhaps the story unfolds from the image and information on the cover in the manner of Raymond Roussel's *La Vue*, *Le Concert*, and *La Source*, whose stories evolved successively from "descriptions" of a miniature image of a beach resort set in a penholder, an engraved vignette of a band concert on hotel letterhead, or a depiction of a spa on the label of a mineral water bottle. Returning to its beginning, Olde Wolbers' story coils in on itself like the mechanical snakes that roil throughout various sequences of her video. Snakes figure within the narrative in different ways but here I am referring to the mythic image of the snake, the ouroboros or African Aidophedo that swallows its own tail and forms a circle, a symbol of eternal return. *Deadline* describes a circle in its voyage, though one that was begun before setting off by taxi or airplane. That is why the circle is also a return to origins, but origins that are always divided.

In a symmetry of beginnings and endings, the narrator
was "welcomed by the exact same man who had earlier
waved me off," who we learn are actually two men: the
narrator's uncle and father respectively. Her father and
uncle were discrepant twins, born at the same time to
one father but two mothers. Chance intervened to
determine who was firstborn and to set their lives of
unequal status on course, their "fate sealed by a mere
guess." What starts out as equal or like – a mirror reflec-
tion of each other – deviates through fate or swerves
through acts of chance. Likewise, the complex family
tree is branched like the bifurcations of the narrative
while partially producing the story's complications as
well. Thus, the first half of the narrative outlines the
family situation filled in with the stories and local legends
that Olde Wolbers gathered during a two-week stay in a
Gambian fishing village. The first part of the narrative
subtly weaves these stories through the fated divergences
of the two brothers. (As in *Trailer*, the artists says, "the
life-long secrets or unspoken feuds that exist in families"
are determinant, "but whereas in the West there are quite
a few things that can be done to change one's situation,
in The Gambia one wrong decision or change of fate can
be a life-long circumstance.")

We find that familiar patterns, derived from African tex-
tiles, hairstyles, and architecture, entwine these stories
and embed them in one another, both visually and within
its narrative figures. For instance, concerning the latter,
the scene of the serial *mis-en-abyme* of the narrator's
uncle's wives, girlfriends, and fiancés "arranged in
fading order of engagement, photographed against

the yellow backdrop upon which they now hung, posing on the same tan leather couch from where I was watching them, the last in the series was a photo of the sofa itself." But as much as spatial, these regressions are temporal, for instance, for her adoptive grandmother, for whom, like Alice's White Queen (who lives backwards), "events furthest in her past are freshest in her memory." Linear regression may only be a cross-section as "generations coiled into one another like rings around a tree."

These patterns (of the circle and *mise-en-abymic* mirroring and regression) repeat in the second half of the story in the father's failed attempt to get to Greece, the voyage proper: in the circling or reversing taxi with its odometer counting backwards; where chance intervenes again in the (magical) shape of the rabbit; in the premonition of meeting the uncle in the personage of Simgam's boss, etc. Simgam's story function is to supply the narrator Salingding (who only receives her name at this point) his deceased wife's Nigerian passport so that she can continue the journey in the place of her father, whose path was interrupted by the unexpected event of the rabbit and its arbitrary legal consequences that prevented him crossing the Nigerian border to catch an airplane in Lagos. Perhaps, the artist speculates, the uncle cast a spell and sent the rabbit to disturb his brother's journey. (As the artist says, "This is also implied in the story when the rabbit is shown again when she meets the uncle at the airport. It refers to West African superstitious beliefs that the uncle somehow made the rabbit appear or even embodied the rabbit." The rabbit incident really happened to Olde Wolber on her trip but, coincidentally, the rabbit image in the video predates the making of *Deadline*.[4] In the story, chance, coincidence, and magic are indistinguishable in their effects.) Salingding assumes another identity or has one thrust upon her. It would be through his daughter's eyes that the father would see this reunion with his estranged sibling. Thus, the separated brothers are united in this roundabout way from the divided origins of their birth.

In contrast to the first half of the narrative where the town was treated as a tourist destination, the second half is a road trip where the characters finally escape the confines of their surroundings. It is also a road movie where destiny is less a destination (a straight line from A to B) than an adventure. As the narrative was a device to collect stories, this film genre acts as vehicle to incorporate random events (picking up picaresque Simgam, striking the rabbit), unusual sights, and fantastic locales such as the upside down netherworld of the gargantuan oil state. A road trip has its rhythms and repetitions, which have been abstracted by the sets of *Deadline*'s image track. In its long boring stretches, the road trip's sights are its sidelines of ornate concrete fences and landscapes that undulate like snakes to the motion of the taxi (and are traced in the gestures of the children's road-game): fertile ground for absent-minded fantasies. Thus, the trip unfurls like a piece of patterned fabric, which can, nonetheless, contain the unexpected, such a fabric being, for instance, Simgam's employer's traditional white lace tunic, which had a "pattern so elaborate that I thought I could see the Eiffel tower in its folds."

Chance, coincidence, magic, family, or the patterns of culture: what shapes these individual lives? Olde Wolbers talks of how the difficulties of this story "highlight the inescapable difference between our mobility and theirs. Most Gambians are trapped in their country like people used to be behind the Iron Curtain." Being trapped in circumstances is a theme of the work, but being trapped is also a structural figure of the narrative: trapped as if in a *mis-en-abyme*. Patterns of accommodation, however, emerge in disguised forms. The disequilibrium of the voyage is pre-figured within fabrics or decorative structures whose repetitive motifs reveal a dissymmetry that belies their seeming static symmetry. Writing about primitive decorative art and face tattooing as figures of social solidarity, Claude Lévi-Strauss says these elements interlock with each other through dislocation, and it is only at the end that the pattern achieves a stability which both conforms and belies the dynamic process according to which it has been carried out. So the traditional and the modern abide together, like the traditional robes of her uncle and the modern garb of her father, or the mythical bush dragon Ninki Nanka and money-spewing snakes emerging from women's vaginas depicted in the hand-painted movie posters for Ghanaian and Nigerian horror films. So dislocation weaves Salingding into her family's ongoing story but now displaced as her father's substitute. Of the brothers, the narrator says, although she could now be speaking of herself, "the fate of their lives could have been so easily swapped. So often hidden behind memory is the undefined relationship with oneself, a vaguely remembered half-stranger ... a parasite." It is just as much this internal doppelgänger, *our* internal *mis-en-abyme*, that sets us on our insane restless journeys. Saskia, too.

116

Notes

1. All the works referred to, other than *Deadline*, are filmed underwater with the sets dipped in paint. Having the appearance of computer-derived imagery, the sets rather are meticulously constructed and filmed.

2. I admit, such an interpretation – that Alfgar has completely made up this story – runs counter to what the artist says on a number of points: "For a long time making this video, I was thinking of Alfgar as being in search of his parents, but in *Trailer* it is his parents who, with the cinema as a vehicle, broadcast the trailer looking for him. I have been fascinated with the way people suddenly discover that they are adopted and that they are not who they thought they were." And: "The jungle images come to his head in the form of memories. He knows that he is really remembering Elmore as his mother, not the actress, because he has only ever seen her in black and white on screen and his memories are in colour. And she never starred in a film in colour." And: "The cashier is his mother, which he finds out when she tells him about Elmore Vella. She uses the third person but he knows it must have been her. How could she have witnessed the unwitnessable? He realizes that she must have been there and therefore that it is his mother operating the very cinema that is like a trap to his past."

3. Olde Wolbers implies that one of the protagonists has already written this book that sets out their exploits.

4. This accounts for the rabbit being filmed underwater.

References

DIKE, CHARLES C., ET AL. "Pathological Lying Revisited,"
The Journal of the American Academy of Psychiatry and the Law,
33:3 (2005), 342-349.

DERRIDA, JACQUES. "History of the Lie," *Without Alibi*, trans.
Peggy Kamuf. Stanford, CA: Stanford University Press, 2002.

FOUCAULT, MICHEL. *The Birth of the Clinic: An Archaeology of
Medical Perception*. New York: Vintage Books, 1973.

FREUD, SIGMUND. "Fragment of an Analysis of a Case of Hysteria,"
Collected Papers, Vol. 3, trans. Alix and James Strachey, New York:
Basic Books, 1959.

LEVI-STRAUSS, CLAUDE. *Triste Tropiques*, trans. John and
Doreen Weightman, New York: Atheneum, 1974.

MONK, PHILIP. *Spirit Hunter: The Haunting of American Culture by
Myths of Violence/Speculations on Jeremy Blake's Winchester Trilogy*.
Toronto: Art Gallery of York University, 2005.

OLDE WOLBERS, SASKIA. Unpublished lecture transcript.

PENFIELD, WILDER, AND PHANOR PEROT. "The Brain's Record
of Auditory and Visual Experience," *Brain*, 86 (1963), 595-696.

SACKS, OLIVER. *The Man Who Mistook His Wife for a Hat*. New York:
Harper & Row, 1985.

WENDL, TOBIAS, "Wicked Villagers and the Mystery of
Reproduction: An Exploration of Horror Movies from Ghana and
Nigeria," *Postcolonial Text*, 3:2 (2007), 1-21.

Deadline
photo archive
Gambia, Benin 2006

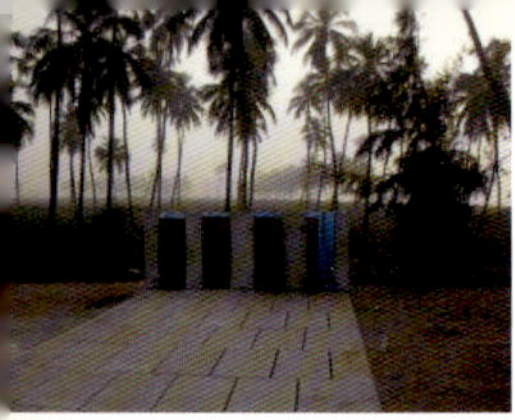

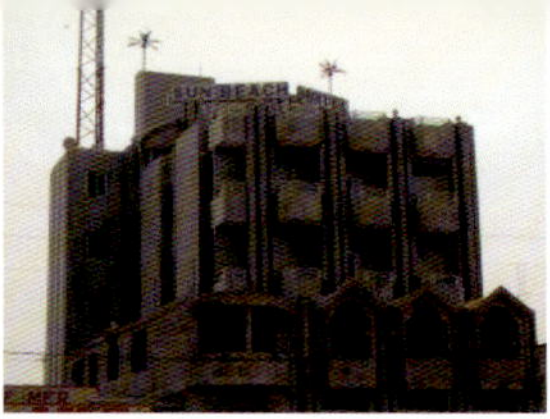

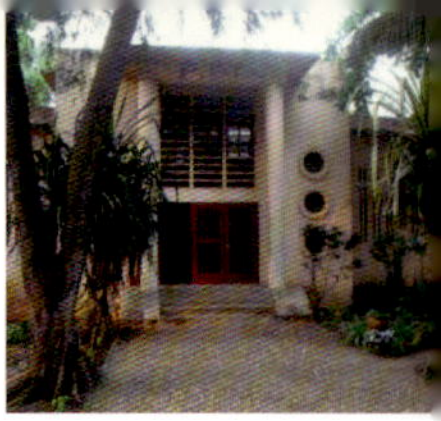

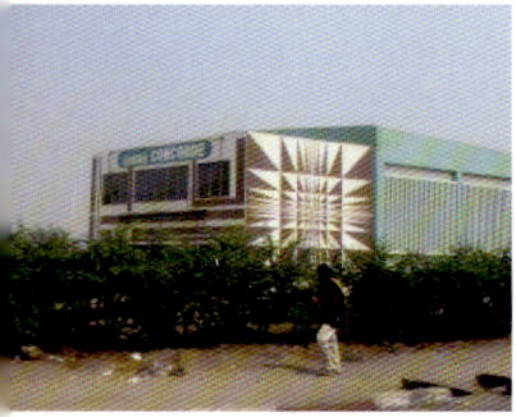

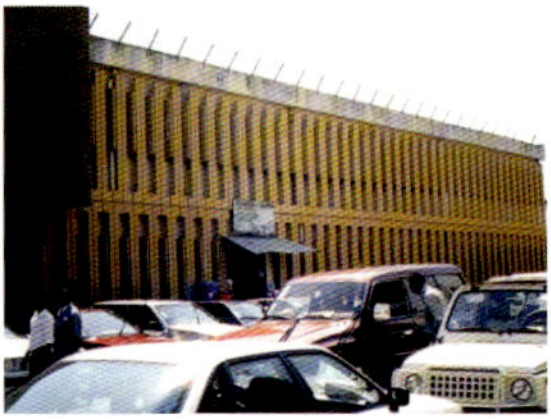

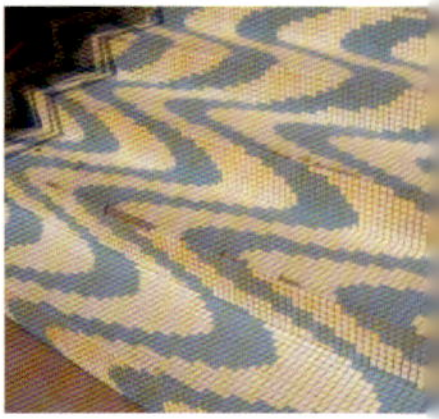

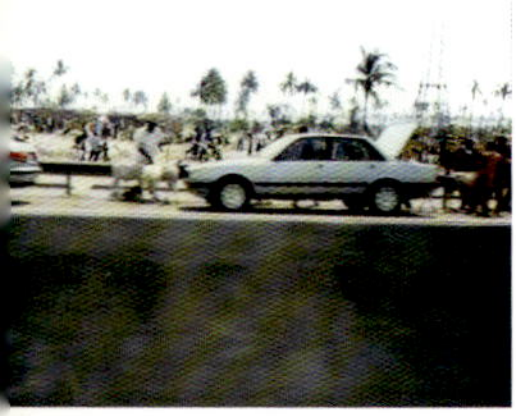

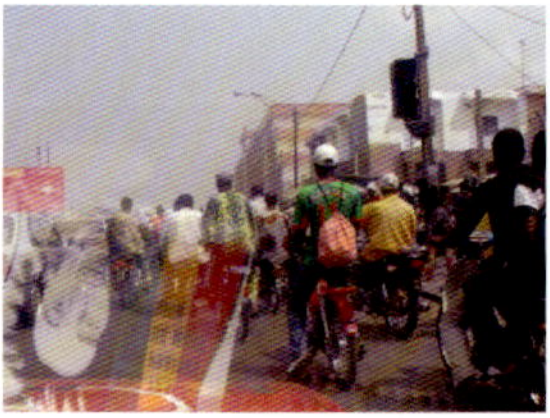

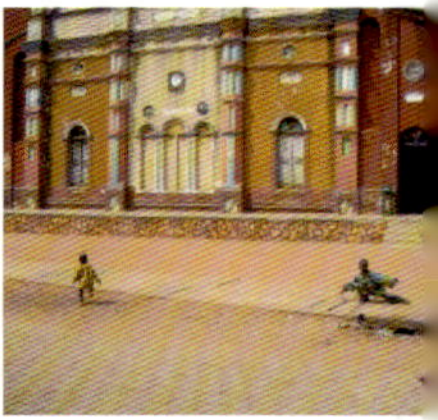

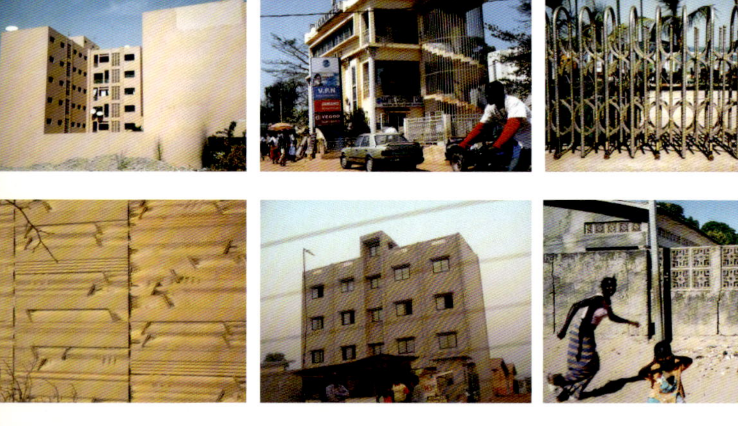
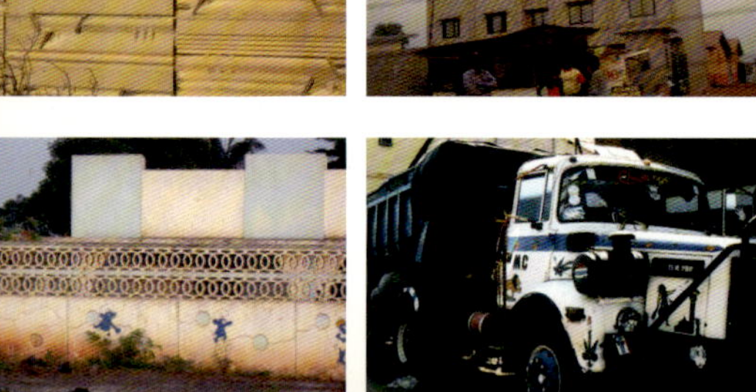

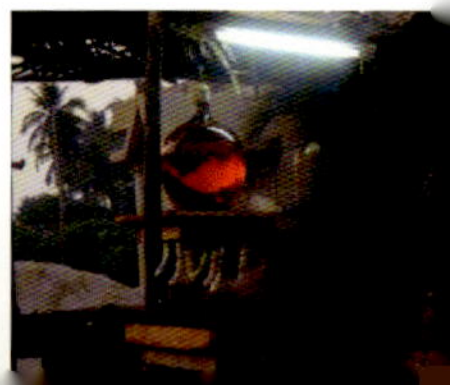

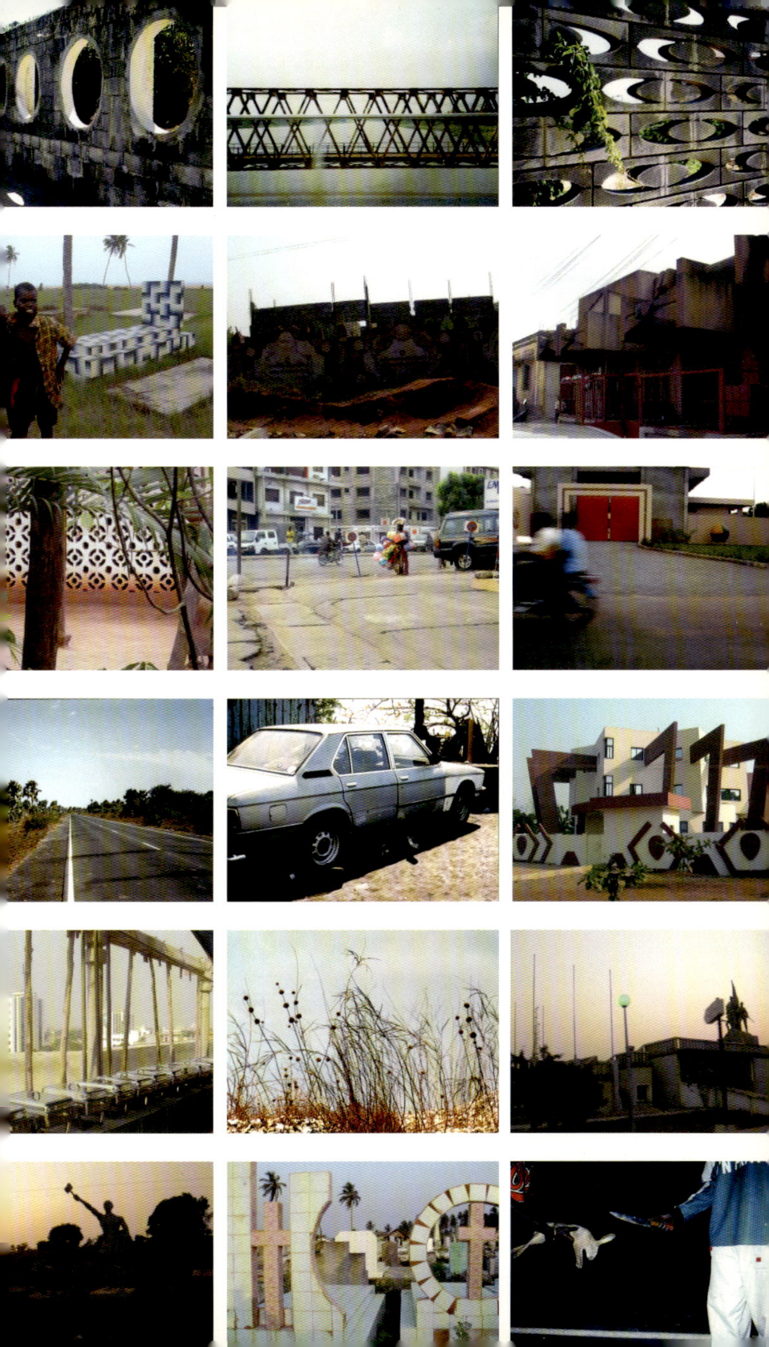

Installations

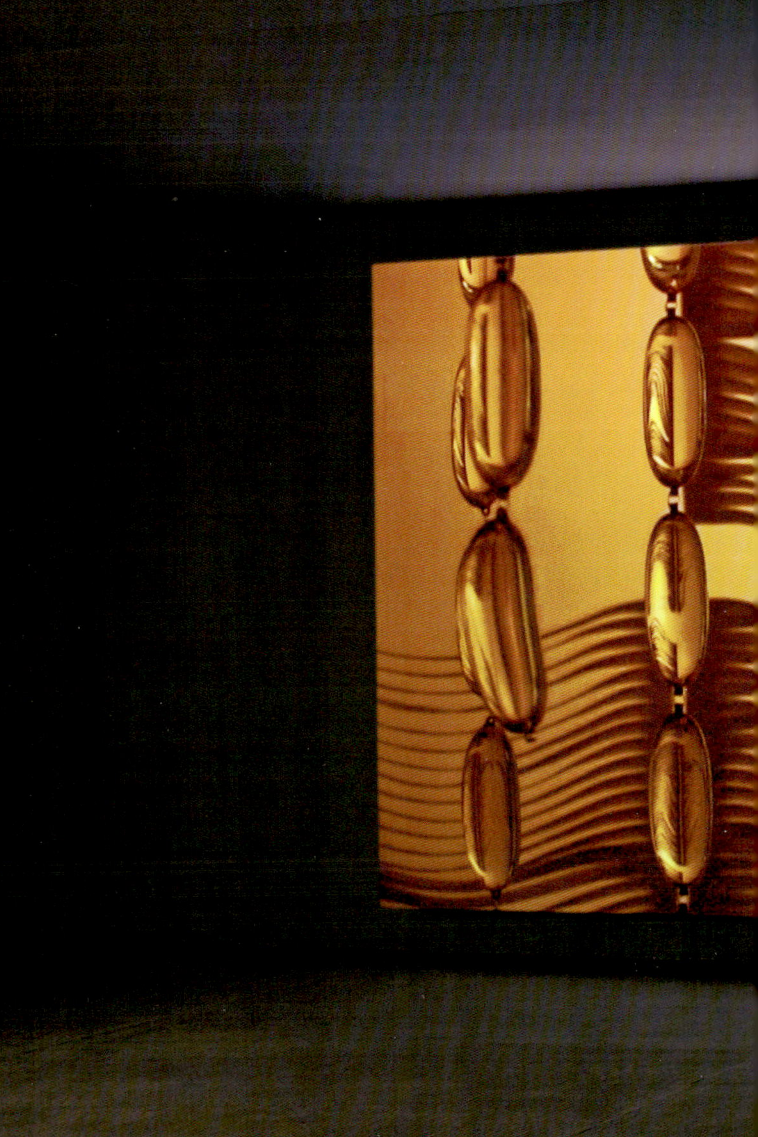

Deadline
installation view
courtesy: Maureen Paley, London

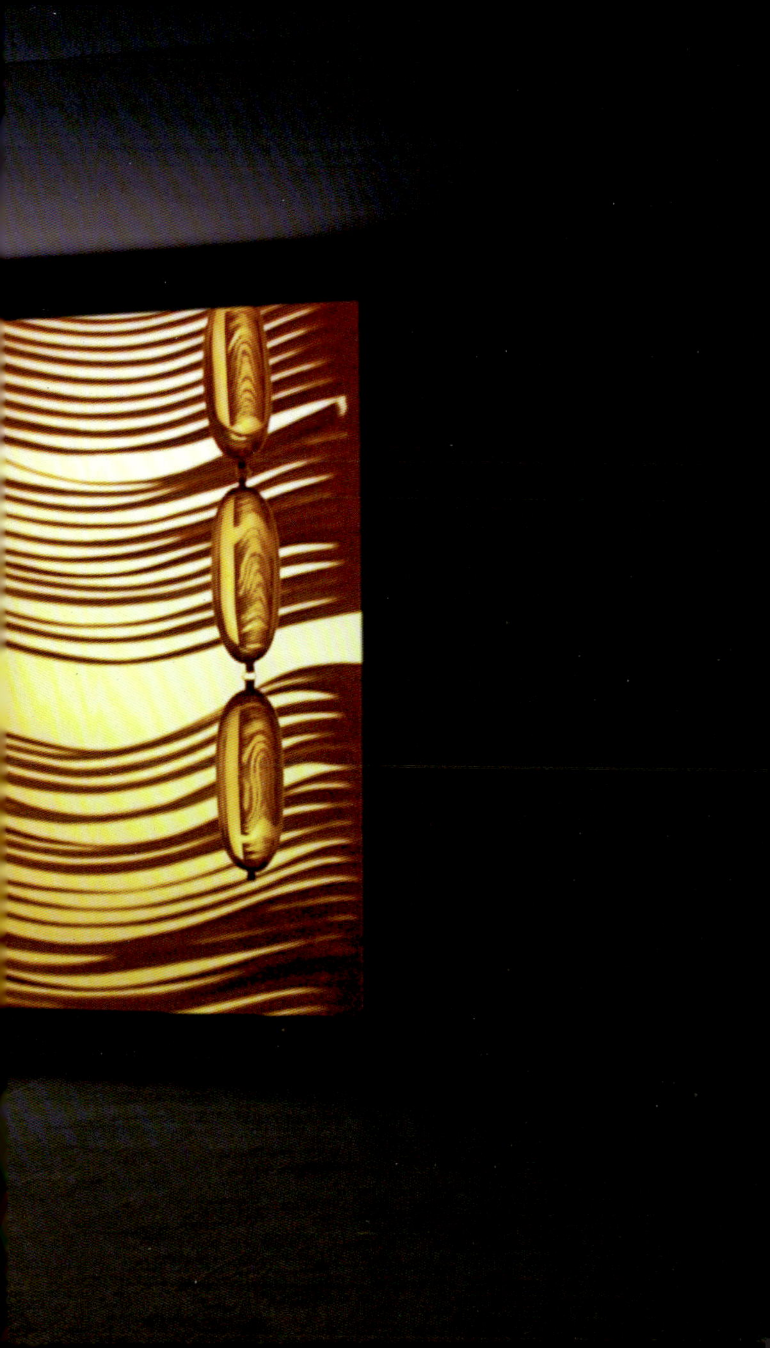

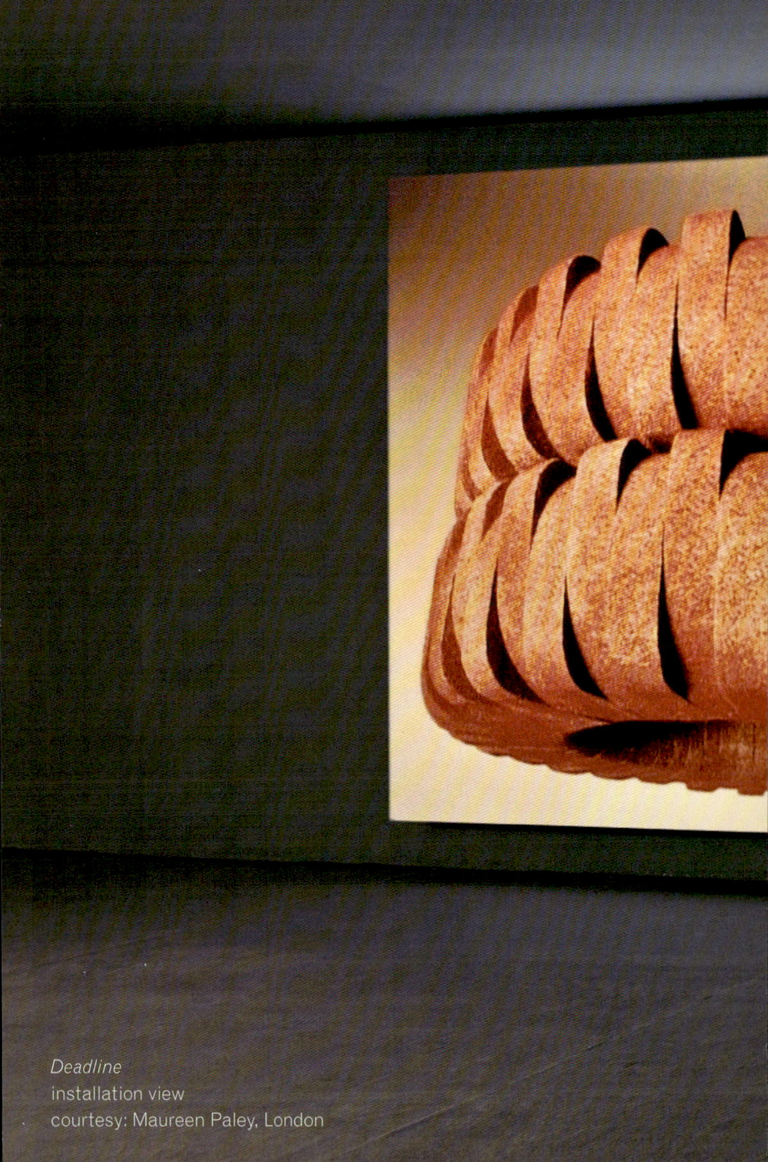

Deadline
installation view
courtesy: Maureen Paley, London

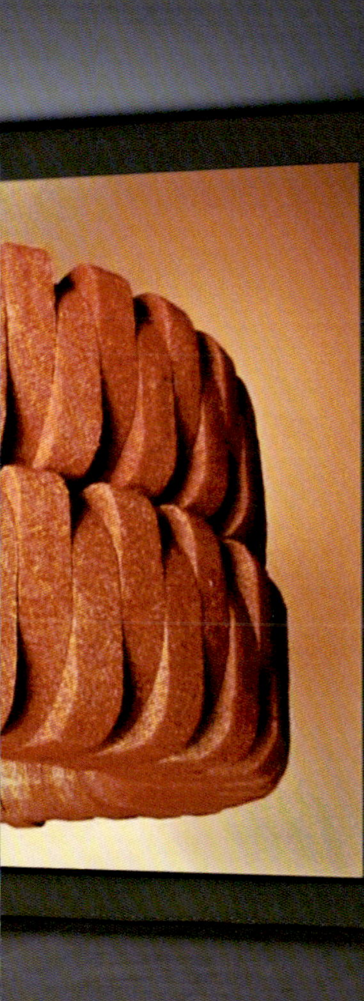

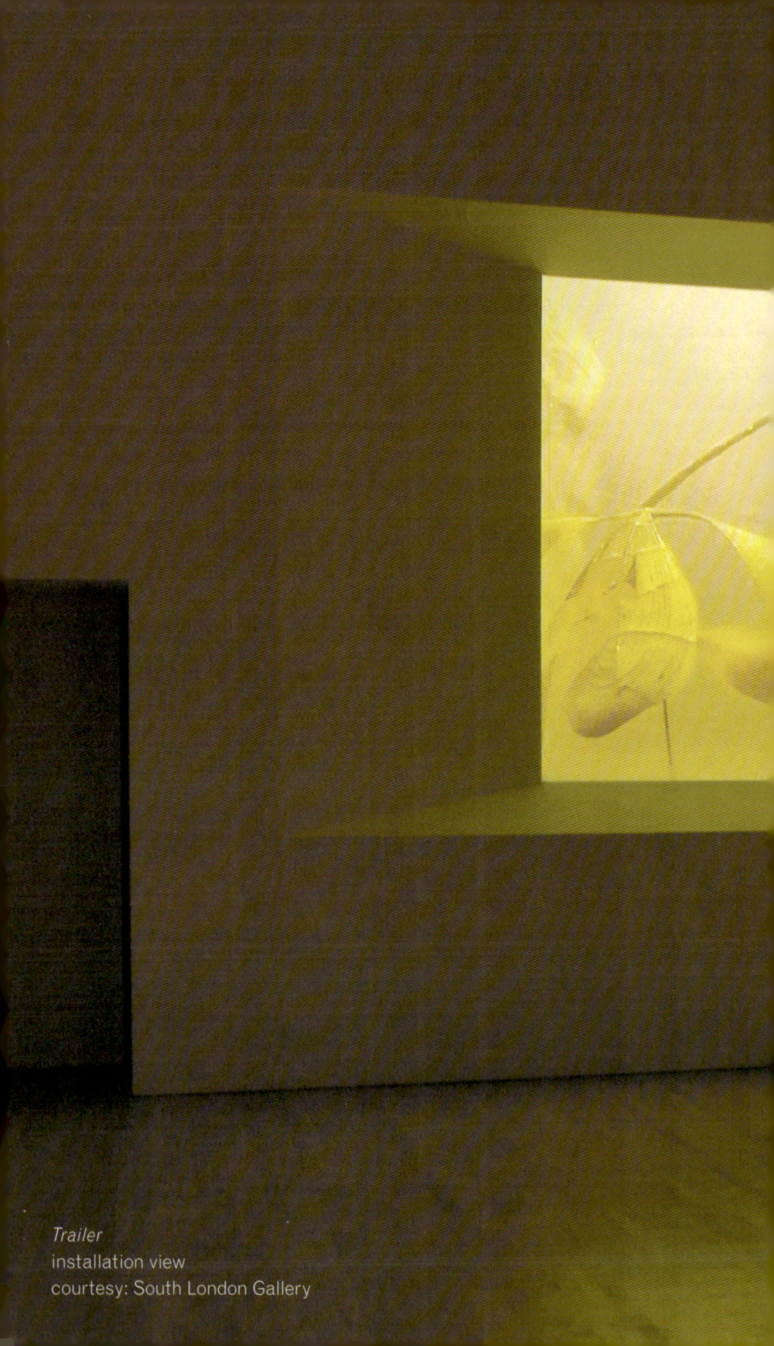

Trailer
installation view
courtesy: South London Gallery

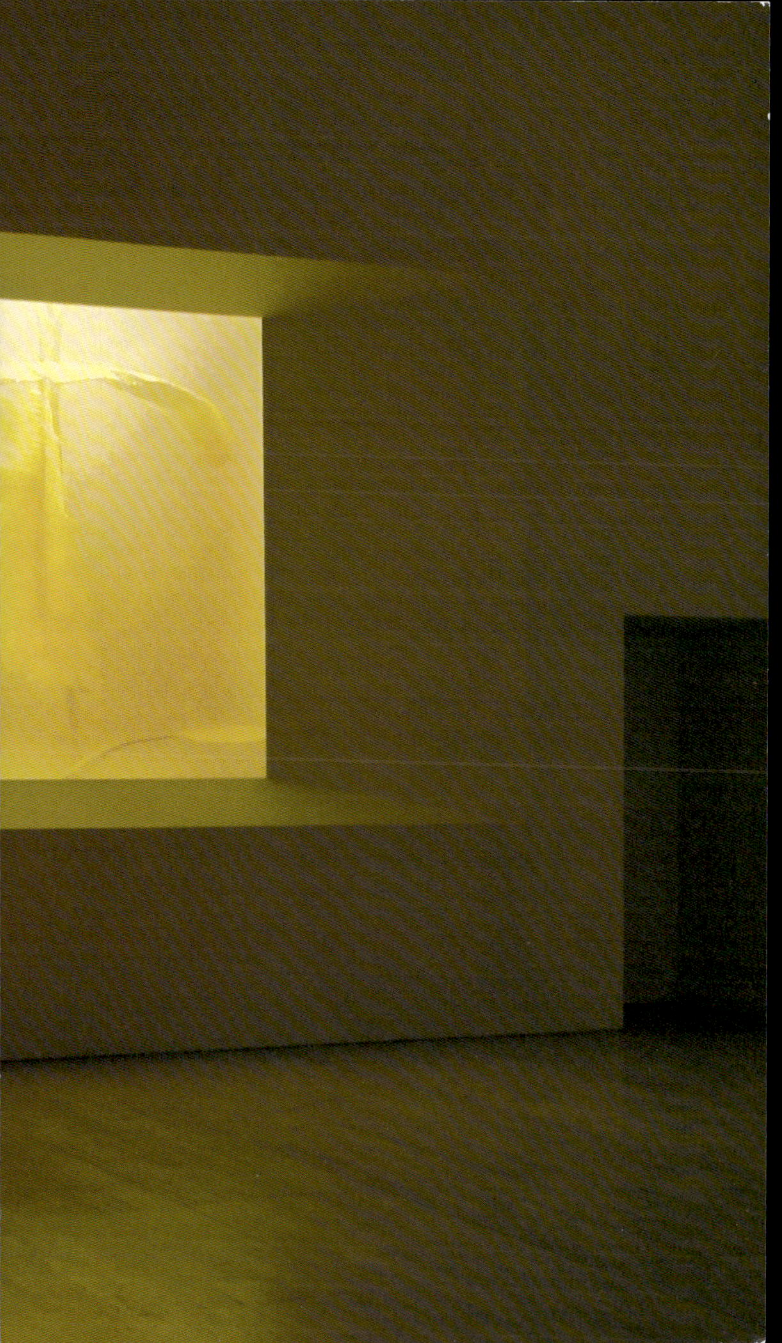

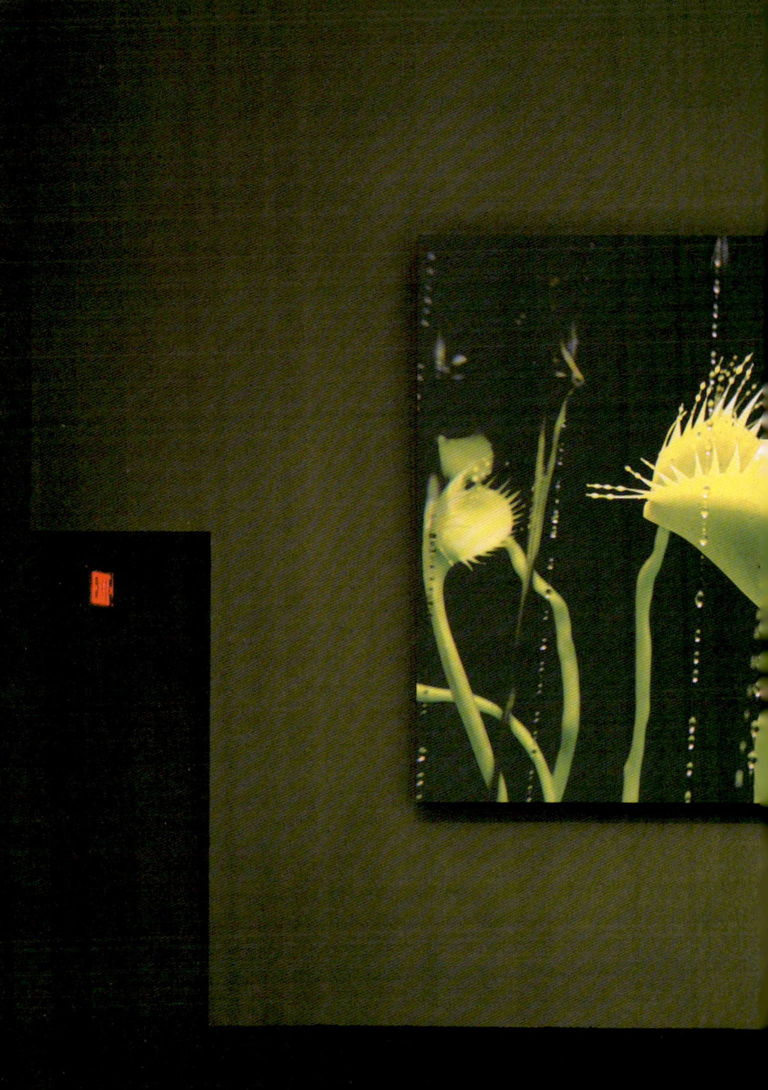

Trailer
installation view
Art Gallery of York University, photo: Cheryl O'Brien

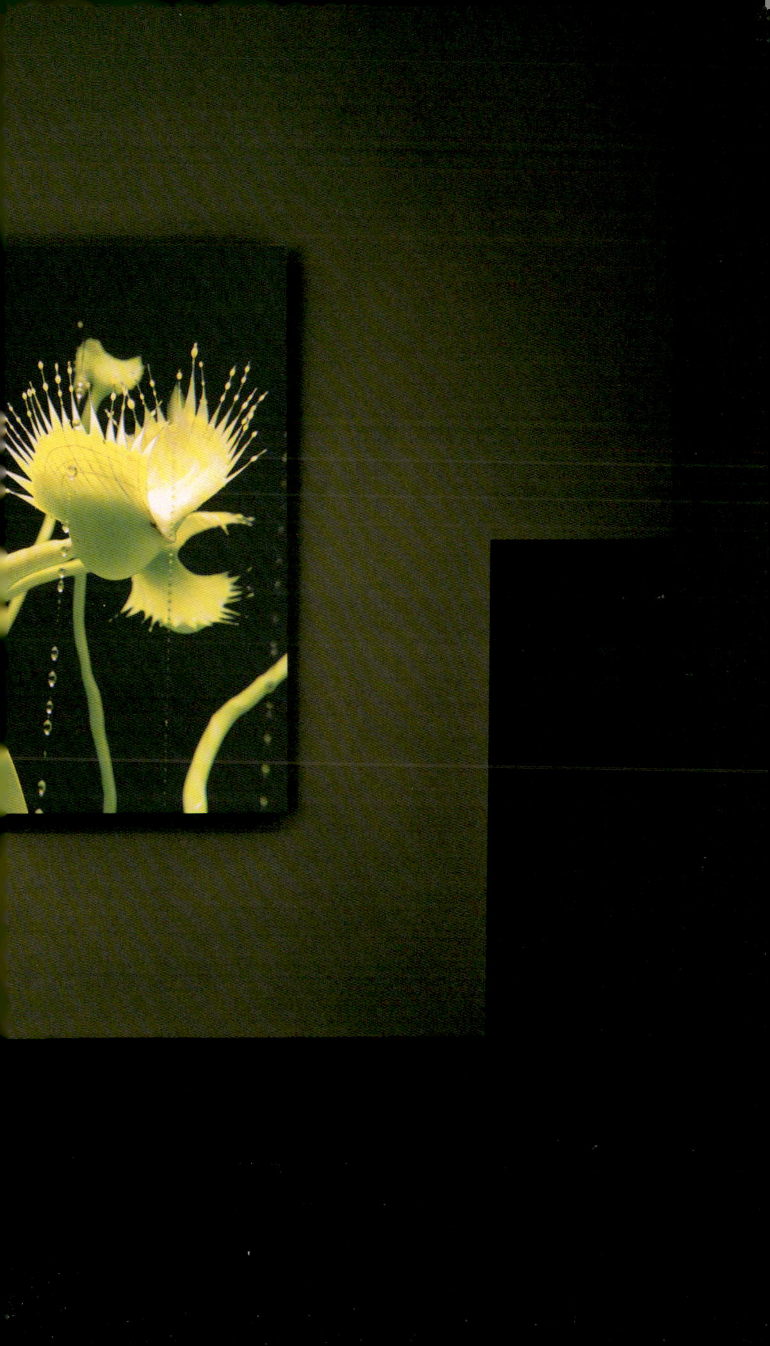

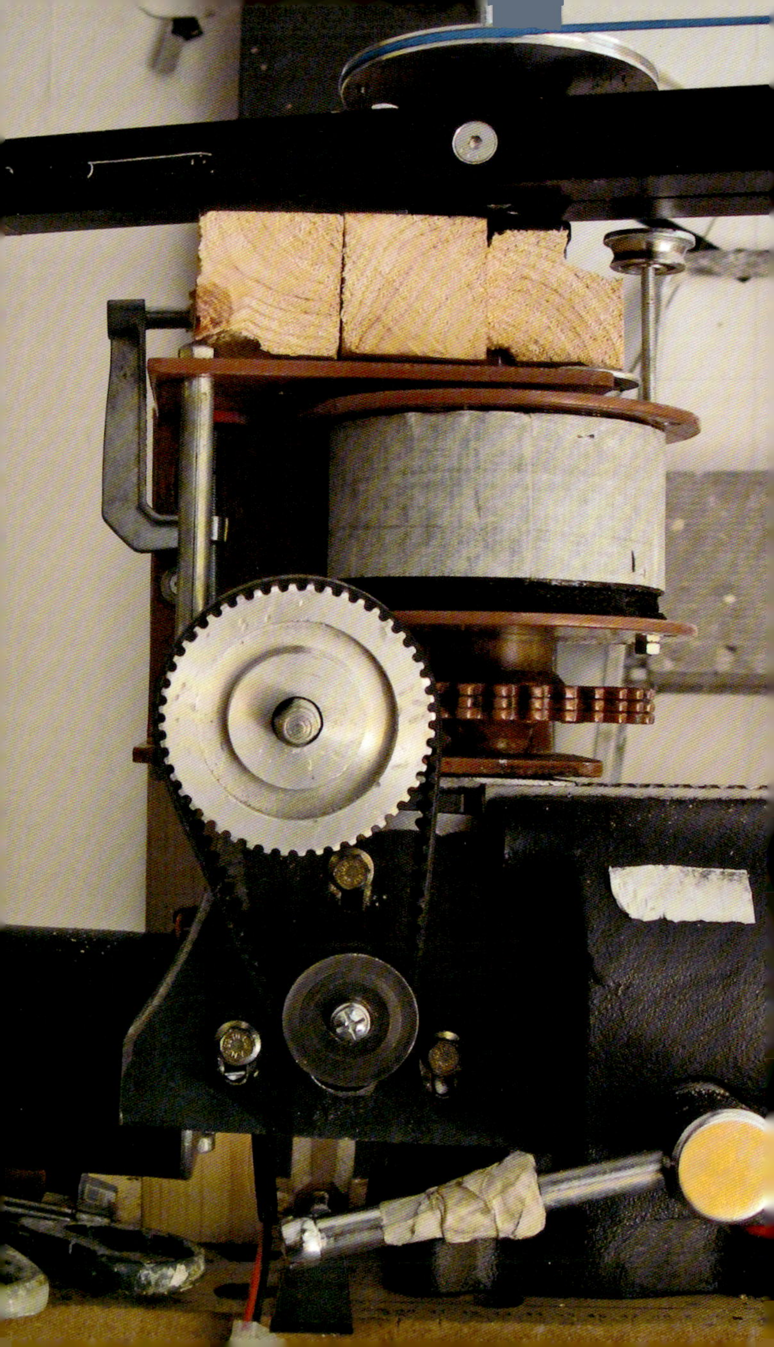

Exhibition
Published in conjunction with an
exhibition of Saskia Olde Wolbers at
the Art Gallery of York University,
6 February – 4 May 2008.
Curated by Philip Monk.
An AGYU Founders Presentation.

Works in the exhibition

Trailer (2005), 10 min DV
Voice-over: John Wynne
Music: Daniel Pemberton
Additional music samples: John Wynne

Deadline (2007), 18 min DV
Voice-over: Kiza Deen
Music: Daniel Pemberton
Additional music samples:
Mory Kante, Gang Gang Dance, John Wynne
Supported by Film London

Deadline: Photographic Archive (2006 – 2007)
Photographs: Cedar Lewisohn, Darragh Hogan,
Patricia Ellis, and Saskia Olde Wolbers

Publication
All works courtesy Maureen Paley, London
Images of Saskia Olde Wolbers' studio
(opposite and overleaf), C-type photographs
of sets, and video stills all courtesy of the artist.

Designed by Bryan Gee
Edited by Michael Maranda
Printed and bound in Canada by Warren's Waterless Printing

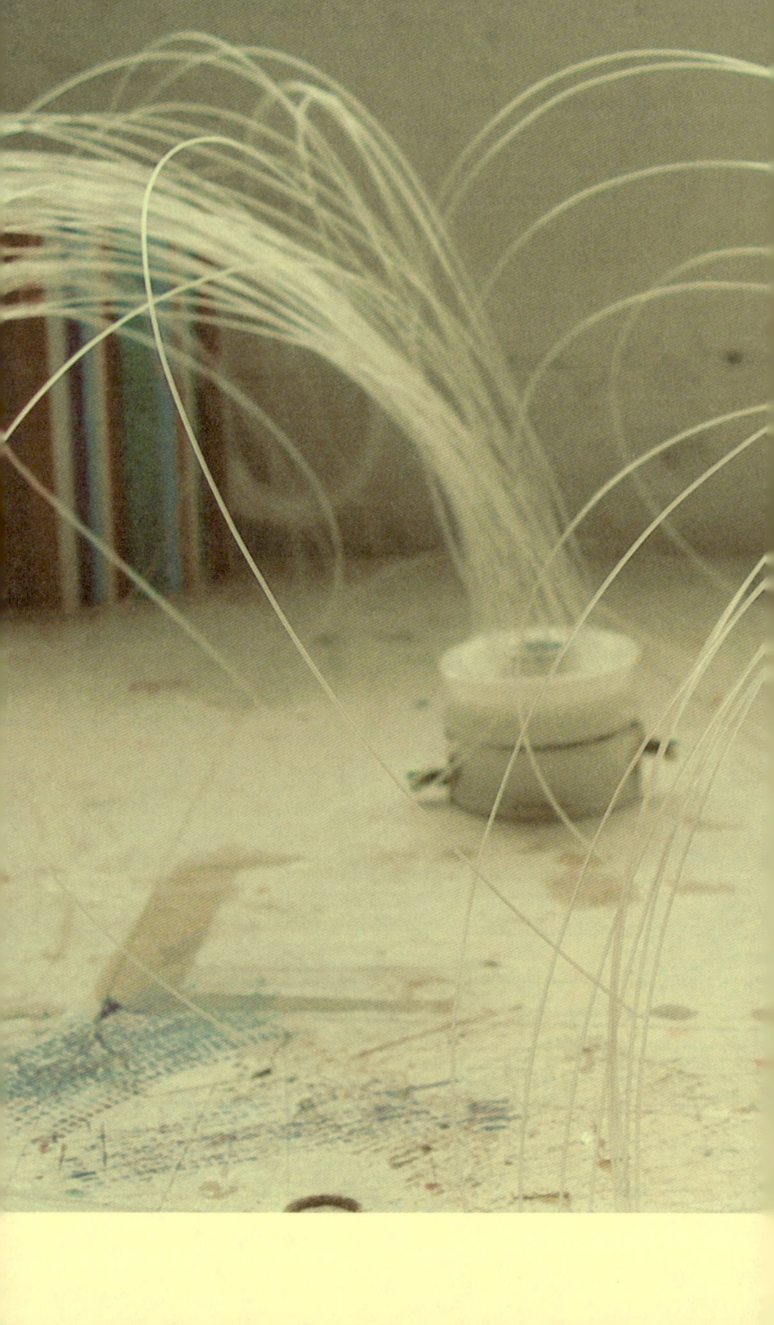

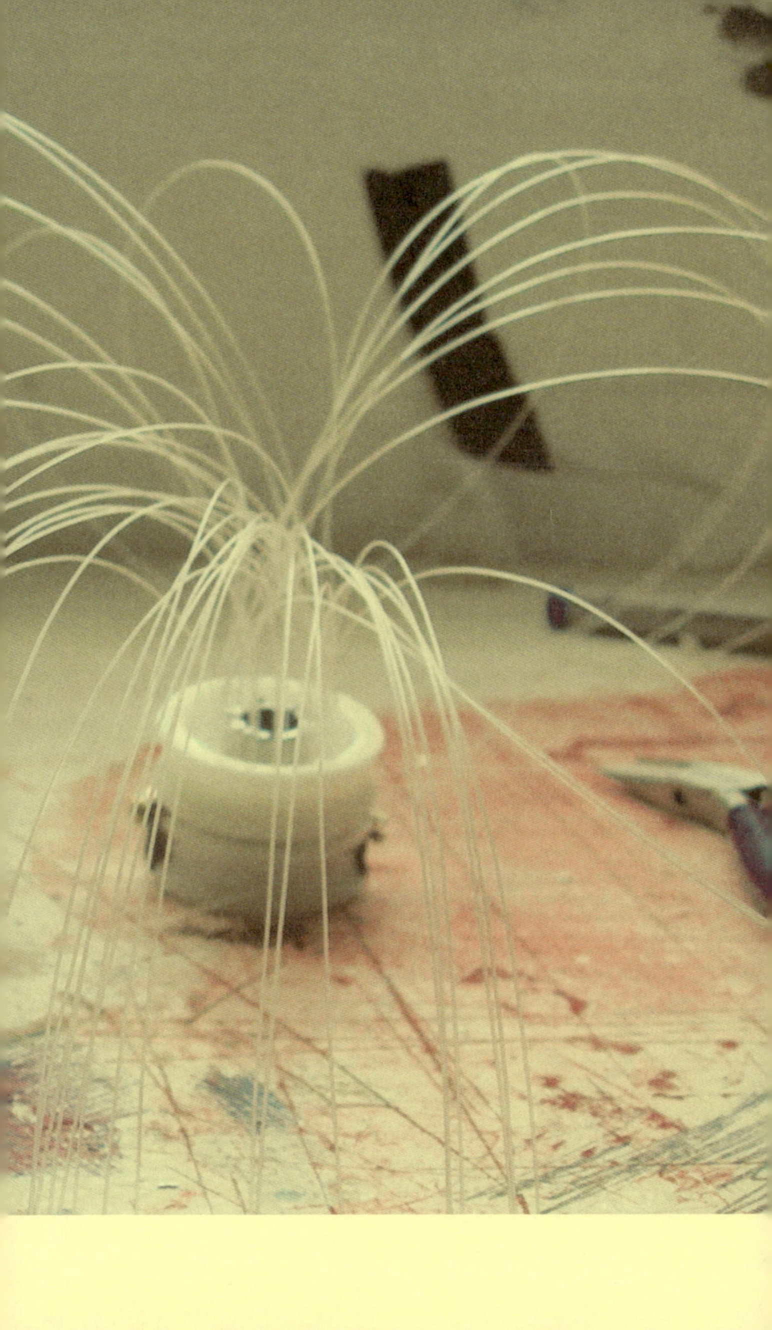

agYU

Art Gallery of York University
4700 Keele St, Toronto ON, Canada. M3J 1P3
www.yorku.ca/agyu

The Art Gallery of York University is supported by
York University, the Canada Council for the Arts,
the Ontario Arts Council, and the City of Toronto
through the Toronto Arts Council.

Acknowledgements
The publication of *and while I have been lying here perfectly still*
is generously supported by the Mondriaan Foundation, Amsterdam.

Conseil des Arts
du Canada

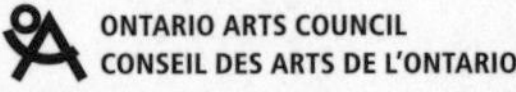

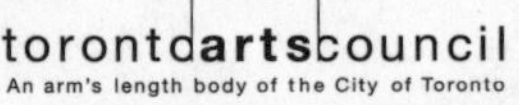

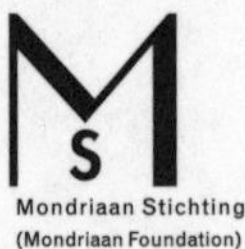